BIKE
REPAIR
MANUAL

CHRIS SIDWELLS

LONDON, NEW YORK, MUNICH,
MELBOURNE, DELHI

Senior Editor Richard Gilbert
Editorial Assistant Satu Fox
Project Art Editor Keith Davis

Jacket Designer Chris Gould
Producer Adam Stoneham

Photographer Gerard Brown

Managing Editor Stephanie Farrow
Managing Art Editor Lee Griffiths

**Original edition produced for
Dorling Kindersley by
Editor** Pip Morgan
Designers Edward Kinsey, Peter Laws
Technical Consultant Guy Andrews

First published in 2004 by
Dorling Kindersley Limited. Published with minor
revisions in 2005, this edition fully revised and
updated in 2008, and with updates in 2011, 2012
by Dorling Kindersley Limited, 80 Strand,
London WC2R 0RL

A Penguin Company

is available from the British Library.

ISBN 978-1-4093-6524-2

Reproduced by Colourscan in Singapore.
Printed and bound by Leo.

See our complete catalogue at
www.dk.com

Contents

Introduction

A clean, well-maintained bike will work efficiently and safely, and add to your enjoyment of cycling by giving you peace of mind.

Safety and efficiency are closely linked. If your gears are not shifting correctly, for instance, they will not only affect your riding efficiency, but also tempt you to look down at them while riding to see what is causing the problem. As a result, you might take your eyes off what is happening on the road ahead and expose yourself to the possibility of a collision. The *Bike Repair Manual* will help you avoid such problems by demonstrating how to maintain your bike regularly and correctly.

Understanding technology

Modern bikes may seem complicated and the technology that manufacturers use may be more sophisticated than ever. However, cycle components work, as they have always done, according to logical principles, so there is no reason for you to be daunted.

Before you begin to service a particular component of your bike, first become familiar with the part by turning to the relevant section. Knowing how a part works makes it easier to maintain.

Above all, be confident and patient with what you are doing. Even if you do not think of yourself as mechanically minded, you may come to enjoy bike maintenance after a time and will certainly enjoy the trouble-free cycling that rewards your efforts.

Collecting information

If you buy a new bike, make sure that you keep the accompanying owner's manual, so that you can refer to it alongside this book. Do the same with any new equipment that you buy.

If your bike is not new, obtain a manual from a bike shop or the manufacturer's web site. Manuals will help you to be aware of the particular maintenance requirements of all the components on your bike.

If you want to learn more about bike mechanics, there are many magazines available that contain tips on specific components. However, the large majority of people who are simply interested in learning how to maintain their bike will find everything they need to know in the pages of the *Bike Repair Manual*.

Using this book

The different maintenance requirements of the most common types of bike are listed at the beginning of the book. These requirements are covered in the step-by-step pages that are specific to the components fitted to each type of bike – for example, suspension forks for mountain bikes.

You will also find a timetable for servicing the parts of your bike and a troubleshooting chart to help you identify and solve problems. The book helps you to spot danger signs and to carry out routine safety checks. These features detail what you need to do and refer you to the relevant step-by-step sequences to explain how to do it.

GETTING
TO KNOW
YOUR BIKE

Understanding your bike will make it easier
to maintain. Identify all the different parts
and components to help you see how they
work together as a whole.

The basic bike

Modern bikes, such as the hybrid bike (*below*), are designed to be light and user-friendly. Each part performs a key function in the overall operation of the bike.

The frame is the skeleton on to which all components are fitted. The fork holds the front wheel, and connects to the handlebars so the bike can be steered. Suspension forks improve comfort and control over rough surfaces. The drivetrain is the system that transfers the rider's energy, via the pedals and cranks, to the rear wheel. It also contains a number of cogs, known as chainrings and sprockets, which carry the chain.

The mechs (also known as derailleurs) change gear by moving the chain on to different chainrings and sprockets. They are controlled by the gear-shifters, which are mounted on the handlebar to allow quick and easy use by the rider. The brakes are

Hybrid bike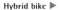
Advances in technology have refined the design and improved the performance of each category of bike part, producing a machine that is easy to ride and maintain.

Wheel (*see pp.110–11, 114–20*)
The rim's shape and high-tech aluminium increases the wheel's strength. Wheels with disc brakes, shown here, can have lighter rims than bikes with rim brakes.

Mech (*see pp.60–5*)
Mechs are designed to cope with the wide range of sprocket sizes required to climb and descend the steepest hills.

Frame (*see pp.12–13*)
Improved welding techniques allow thin-walled aluminium tubes to provide a relatively cheap, light and responsive frame. The thickness of the tube walls varies to cope with areas of increased stress.

Pedal (*see pp.88–95*)
Clipless pedals allow more power to be transferred to the wheels because the feet are fixed to the pedals. Flat pedals, and toe clips and straps, are simpler, but easier to use.

Drivetrain (*see pp.66–87*)
Stiff materials maximize the amount of power the drivetrain transfers to the rear wheel. A triple chainset increases gear range and a flexible chain allows quick, easy gear-shifts.

controlled by brake levers that are also mounted on the handlebar, and use brake pads to press against the wheel's rim, or discs attached to the hub, to stop the bike.

High-tech machine ▶
Many years of design refinement have produced an adaptable hybrid bike, which combines technology from road and mountain bikes for use in an urban environment.

Gear-shifters
(see pp.52–9)
Ergonomically designed gear shifters were developed from mountain bikes, and give easy, precise gear-shifts.

Fork (see pp.150–61)
Forks are designed with varying thickness in the tube wall. Tubes are thin in the middle and thick at both ends. This reduces weight and absorbs road shock. Some forks also act as suspension systems, further reducing shock and improving control.

Brake (see pp.120–47)
Disc brakes offer sensitive, powerful braking that is not affected by weather conditions. Other bikes have rim brakes, which are still very good, although they require earlier braking to slow in the wet.

Tyre (see pp.116–17)
Modern tyres are made from rubber compounds that roll well on the road, while adhering to it when cornering. They often have puncture-resistant bands of material, such as Kevlar, beneath the tread.

Anatomy of the bike

Understanding how the parts on your bike fit together will help you perform maintenance tasks successfully. Although your bike may differ from the modern mountain bike (*right*), all bikes fit together in a similar way. For example, the quick-release levers on the wheels below perform the same function as axle nuts on a bike with hub gears.

The main parts and their components, and where each part is attached to the bike, are shown on the mountain bike. Take the time to study the illustration, since it will act as a useful reference to help you follow the steps later in the book.

Mountain bike ▶

The mountain bike is a good example of how parts fit together since it has a similar frame, wheels, drivetrain, pedals, mechs, brakes, and gear-shifters to road and hybrid bikes.

Saddle
Saddle cover
Saddle rails

Seat post
Saddle clamp

Rear brake
Cable-guide tube
Braking surface
Brake pad
Brake arm

Frame
Seat tube
Seat stay
Chainstay
Down tube

Rear hub
Rear drop-out
Hub
Quick-release

Bottom bracket

Cassette
Cassette body
Sprocket
Locknut

Rear mech
Jockey wheel
Mech plate
Barrel adjuster

Bike controls

Gear-shifter
Handlebar
Grip
Brake lever

Steering

Handlebar stem
Top cup and bearing
Spacer
Stem cap
Head tube
Top tube
Steerer tube
Bottom cup and bearing

Fork crown
Fork leg
Slider

Quick-release

THE ASSEMBLED BIKE

Bike parts are designed to bolt together in the same way to allow straightforward maintenance by following a few key workshop principles (*see pp.34–5*). Most parts use Allen bolts, so for many tasks an Allen key multi-tool is all that is required.

Front wheel

Hub
Spoke
Rim

Tyres

Tyre bead
Valve
Tyre
Inner tube

Drivetrain

Right-hand crank
Chainring
Front mech
Chain

Pedal

Pedal body
Foot retention mechanism
Pedal axle

Bikes for general use

You can buy a bike for almost every purpose imaginable but a simple utility, hybrid, or folding bike will still increase your fitness, save you money on fares, and make no negative impact on your environment.

    As long as the bike is of good quality, you will only need to keep it clean and check it regularly for signs of wear. Hybrid bikes, utility bikes, and folding bikes are all dependable machines that are suited to commuting to work or school, day-to-day transport needs, or simply a pleasurable ride in the park or even the countryside.

The hybrid bike

Lightweight materials combined with road bike performance and hardy mountain bike technology make hybrid bikes perfect for bumpy urban roads. They are ideal for commuting, family rides, fitness riding, touring, and carrying luggage.

The utility bike

Utility bikes are ideal for local commuting and short rides. They are equipped with fat tyres that absorb road bumps but will drag on long journeys, making them hard work to ride and uncomfortable.

The folding bike

Ideal for commuters, and for people with little space in which to store a standard bike, folding bikes can go anywhere, especially on public transport. The folded bike can be easily reassembled into a serviceable machine without the use of tools.

Urban commuting
With its head-up, traffic-friendly riding position and easy-to-operate gears, the lightweight hybrid is ideal for urban commuting.

ESSENTIAL MAINTENANCE CHECKLIST
HYBRID BIKE

• Regularly maintain and lubricate the derailleur gears (see pp.62–3, 64–5).
• Check the gear cables for signs of wear (see p.47, pp.58–9).
• Check the brake cables or hoses, and pads for signs of wear (see p.47, pp.126–7).
• Check the tyres for signs of wear (see p.47).
• Regularly change the chain (see pp.72–3).

Tyre

Rear mech

Front mech

Gear cable

Brake cable

Chain

UTILITY BIKE

• Regularly lubricate the hub gears (see pp.68–9).
• Regularly check the gear cables for signs of wear (see p.47).
• Regularly check the brake control cables for signs of wear (see pp.126–7).
• Regularly check the brake pads for signs of wear (see p.46).
• Regularly clean and grease the chain (see pp.36–9).

Handlebar basket

Sprung saddle

Brake lever

Hub gears

Chainguard

FOLDING BIKE

• Regularly check and lubricate the pivots and the locks that allow the bike to fold and unfold.
• Regularly check hub gears, even though they are shielded from the elements and so need very little maintenance (see pp.68–9).
• Pay extra attention to the outer control cables (see p.47, pp.58–9).

Rear suspension

Hub and derailleur gear system

Folded bike

Frame hinge

Large chainrings

Unfolded bike

Specialist bikes

If you want to take up cycling as a sport or hobby, rather than simply as a means of transport, look for a more specialized bike, such as a race-level road bike, a mountain bike, or a triathlon bike.

As bikes become more sophisticated they need more care. For example, lightweight parts wear quickly, so they must be kept scrupulously clean. Carbon wheel rims require special brake pads that do not work well on metal. Hydraulic disc brakes and suspension systems need regular attention. Electronic gear systems need their batteries recharged.

Do not let this put you off buying your dream bike. Just as riding it will be a joy, maintaining it to exacting standards will be part of the whole cycling experience.

The road bike

Lightweight materials and narrow tyres make road bikes good for fitness riding, day touring, and competitions. The aerodynamic position afforded by a drop handlebar offers great speed. Road bikes are so light and have such a range of gears that almost anyone, with a little training, can tackle the great mountain passes made famous by the Tour de France.

The mountain bike

Full-suspension mountain bikes allow you to break new ground and ride across rugged terrain that was previously unthinkable and at speeds that were once unattainable.

The triathlon and time-trial bike

This type of bike is used in triathlons and time-trial races, where competitors cannot draft behind each other, so the bike must be as aerodynamic as possible. The bike's geometry allows the rider to get low and narrow, smoothing the air flow over them.

Road riding
This road bike represents the ultimate in road bike design, and is the type of bike that professionals use in the Tour de France.

ESSENTIAL MAINTENANCE CHECKLIST
ROAD BIKE

- Regularly clean and lubricate the bike (see pp.36–9).
- Make routine safety checks (see pp.40–1).
- Check the brakes (see pp.128–9).
- Check the gears are working perfectly (see pp.62–5).
- Check frame protector pads for wear in the locations where cable outers touch carbon-fibre frames (see p.41).

Calliper brake

Electronic gear-shift system

Carbon-fibre frame

Aluminium drop handlebar

Road race tyre

Clipless pedal

Lightweight wheels

MOUNTAIN BIKE

- Set up the suspension fork and rear shock (see pp.152–9, 164–5).
- Regularly clean and lubricate the suspension (see pp.160–1).
- Regularly inspect pivots (see pp.166–7) and seals.
- Check brake cables or hoses, and pads (see pp.46–7, 126–7, 138–9).
- Replace the cassette every six months (see pp.76–7).
- Service the headset regularly (see pp.100–3).

Rear shock

Rear derailleur

Carbon-fibre frame

Straight handlebar

Wheels come in both 26- and 29-inch sizes

Suspension fork

Disc brake

TRIATHLON AND TIME-TRIAL BIKE

- Regularly inspect the frame and any carbon-fibre wheels for signs of cracks (see pp.40–1).
- Tyres on tri-bikes are light and thin – check them for cuts, splits and bulges (see p.47).
- Check that the gears are shifting perfectly, and replace cables if necessary (see pp.56–7).
- Maintain and adjust brakes so they can be applied with minimum force (see pp.128–9).

Aerodynamic frame

Carbon-fibre disc wheel

Integrated tri-bars for a low, narrow riding position

Electronic bar-end shifters

Deep section carbon-fibre front wheel

Deep chainrings improve air-flow

Bikes for enthusiasts

Many cyclists become enthusiasts for particular kinds of bikes. These bikes might not be designed for different terrains or for competing – rather they might be designs that suit a lifestyle or are fun to ride.

The examples featured here all require general and some specific maintenance, although a big appeal of BMX and fixie bikes is their simplicity of design, making them easy to maintain. Tandems have maintenance needs due to the double load they carry.

The fixie

One of the simplest bikes, fixies have a single "fixed" gear, meaning that the pedals must turn constantly for the wheel to rotate. They are perfect for everyday use and are simple to maintain. Some have a "flip-flop" hub, which also contains a freewheel.

The BMX

BMXs are made for acceleration and agile bike handling. Like some of the very first bicycles, they are made almost entirely from steel because it transfers power in a way that no other material can.

The tandem

A bicycle made for two must be twice as strong, but it is also twice as hard to stop. Brake maintenance is crucial. So is having a well-maintained, smooth-shifting drivetrain.

Riding fixed
Fixies are ideal for all-year-round use – their lack of gears means they can function in all weathers with little maintenance.

ESSENTIAL MAINTENANCE CHECKLIST

BMX

- Regularly check the bottom bracket to see that it is running free, but not loose.
- Replace the pedals if their axles are bent (see pp.90–1).
- Adjust the brakes to ensure the minimum of travel before the brakes come on, as the steel rims, though very strong, do not make good braking surfaces (see pp.134–5).

Gyro headset

Single gearing

Stunt peg

Opposite transmission

FIXIE

- Regularly inspect the bottom bracket, steering, and wheel bearings to check that they are running free but have no play (see pp.82–5, 100–3, 112–13).
- Check that the wheel nuts are tight before each ride (see pp.74–5).
- Check brakes for excessive travel (see pp.128–35).
- Check pedals for damage and wear (see pp.90–1).

Single gear, sometimes with flip-flop hub

Straight handlebar

Large-flange hubs

Deep-section rims

Hard-wearing clipless pedals

TANDEM

- Check brakes for excessive travel and pad wear (see pp.128–35).
- Check the chain for wear, and clean and lubricate it regularly (see pp.36–9, 72–3).
- Check the wheels for trueness and wear – tandem wheels are put under great stress (see pp.118–19).
- Check the longer cable lengths for wear (see p.47).

Pilot's saddle

Robust frame with extra-thick tubes

Pilot's handlebar

Stoker's handlebar

Cantilever brakes

Stoker's saddle

Crossover drivetrain

Two pairs of pedals

Setting up a mountain bike

If the saddle's height and angle are adjusted and the position of the brake levers on the handlebar is set so that they are within easy reach, then riding will be more efficient and comfortable. A novice cyclist should try setting the saddle height a little lower at first, and work towards the ideal once he or she is used to riding.

STEP LOCATOR

Toolbox
- Allen key multi-tool • Spanners
- Screwdriver

Adjusting your riding position

1 **Remove your shoes** and sit on your bike, supporting yourself against a wall.

- Set your cranks so that the pedal furthest from the wall is at the low point of its revolution.

- Put the heel of your foot on the pedal. Your leg should be straight when you do this. Ask someone to help you check.

The knee aligns with the axle

4 **Place the widest part** of your foot over the pedal axle. If your shoes have cleats, set them up so that your foot can easily adopt this position (see pp.94–5).

- Set your cranks parallel to the floor. The depression on the side of your leading leg, just behind the kneecap, should be directly over the axle of the pedal. Ask your helper to check.

5 **Move your saddle back** if the depression on your leg is in front of the axle. If it is behind, move it forwards.

- Undo the saddle clamp under the saddle. On modern bikes, you will need an Allen key; on older bikes, use a spanner.

- Repeat Steps 4 and 5 until you are sure you have the position right.

Raise the saddle if your leg is not straight when your heel is on the pedal. Lower the saddle if your heel does not reach the pedal.

● Undo the seat pin clamp bolt. Raise or lower the saddle, tighten up the bolt, and try again. Ask your helper to see if your leg is straight. Do not lean on the foot that you are testing.

To make absolutely sure the saddle height is right for you, go for a ride with your cycling shoes on and your feet in their normal position on the pedals.

● Ask your helper to ride behind you and check that your hips are not rocking from side to side as you ride. If they are, the saddle is set too high and you need to repeat Steps 1 and 2.

Make sure that the brake reach allows you to apply the brakes using the first joints of your first two fingers, while holding the handlebar securely with your thumb and remaining fingers. You should be able to hook your fingers over the brake levers. If you have to stretch too far, you will be unable to apply the correct power.

Adjust the reach of the brake levers if you have to stretch too far.

● Undo the brake cable (see pp.130–1) and screw in the adjuster on the lever until you can reach it easily. Then reclamp the brake cables.

● Set the brake levers at an angle to the handlebar so that you can pull them in line with your arm.

Setting up a road bike

When setting up your road bike, the aerodynamics of your position is especially important, since road bikes are designed for speed. Your aim is to be efficient so that your pedalling energy is turned into forward motion, and you sit in a way that doesn't impede your progress by increasing drag. You also need to be comfortable and in control.

STEP LOCATOR

Toolbox

- Allen key multi-tool ● Straight edge

Adjusting your riding position

1 **Remove your cycling shoes** and get on your bike, supporting yourself on a wall or with the rear wheel mounted on a turbo trainer.

- Set your cranks so that the pedal furthest from the wall is at the low point of its revolution.

- Sit with your bottom level in the saddle, not favouring either side, and place your heel on the pedal. Your saddle is at the correct height when your leg is straight.

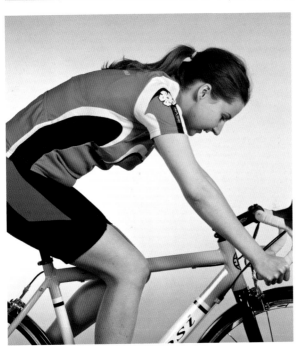

4 **To check your stem length** sit on your bike with your feet on the pedals, holding the bottom of the bar.

- Look down at the front-wheel hub: it should be obscured by the handlebar. If the hub is in front of the bar your stem is too short; if it is behind the bar your stem is too long.

- If you have to change your stem, measure it and work out how much longer or shorter the new stem needs to be. Remove and replace it (see pp.100–1).

- Back-pedal, sitting in the same position: if your upper leg touches your stomach and feels like it will restrict breathing, raise your handlebar. To do this, swap the headset spacers (see pp.100–1) or fit a shallower handlebar (see pp.106–7).

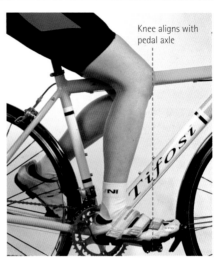

Knee aligns with
pedal axle

2 **Lower your saddle** if your heel doesn't touch the pedal. Raise it if your heel touches the pedal but your leg is bent.

● Undo the seat bolt – an Allen bolt on most road bikes – adjust the saddle height, and retighten it.

● While pedalling, ask someone to stand behind you and check that your hips don't rock up and down with each revolution – a sign that the saddle is too high. Lower the saddle if this occurs.

3 **To set the optimum** fore-and-aft position of your saddle on the seat post, place the widest part of your foot over the pedal axle.

● With your cranks horizontal, the depression on the outside of your knee – just behind the knee cap – should be directly over the pedal axle.

● To achieve this, undo the saddle-clamp bolt under your saddle and shift it forwards or back on the seat post, then retighten the bolt.

5 **The optimum position for brake levers** is for the tip of each lever to line up with the flat section at the bottom of the handlebar.

● Place a straight edge against the underneath of the flat section. Peel back the brake-lever cover to expose the clamp bolt. Loosen it with an Allen key.

● Move the lever up or down to align the lever tip with the straight edge. You may have to remove the handlebar tape to achieve this (see pp.106–7).

6 **Adjust the handlebar angle** until it feels comfortable to ride with your hands on the brake levers, and to apply the brakes while holding the lower section of the handlebar.

● Loosen the stem's handlebar-clamp bolts and twist the handlebar to angle it up or down. The optimum position for you can only be found by trying several different positions, but extreme handlebar angles should be avoided.

Setting up a child's bike

Before a child starts riding a bike, adjust the saddle and handlebar to suit his or her body. Set the saddle at its lowest point, as in Step 1. Buy the biggest bike possible at first, then keep adjusting it as the child grows taller. Children's bikes are usually measured by wheel size – from 30cm (12in) up to 60cm (24in).

STEP LOCATOR

1	1
2	2
3	3

Toolbox
- Allen key multi-tool ● Spanners
- Plastic mallet

Adjusting the position of the saddle

1 **Set the saddle** on your child's bike at a height that allows him or her to sit on it and simultaneously to touch the ground with the front part of each foot. This is the ideal set-up.

Adjusting the height of the handlebar

1 **Raise or lower the bike's handlebar** by loosening the expander bolt that holds the stem into the bike. This bolt is secured by either an Allen bolt or a hexagonal bolt, so use an Allen key or a spanner to loosen it.

● Knock the bolt down with a plastic mallet to free it up if you need to.

2 **Grip the front wheel** between your legs to steady it and then pull the handlebar up or push it down. Do not pull the handlebar higher than the safety limit that is marked on the stem. Once the handlebar is at the right height, and the stem is lined up with the front wheel, tighten the expander bolt.

Loosen the seat pin clamp – it either has a quick-release lever or a nut-and-bolt fixing that requires a spanner. Either pull the saddle up or push it down to the required height.

Move the saddle forwards or backwards by loosening the nut that secures the seat clamp. Tighten the nut again, but be sure that the saddle is horizontal to the ground.

Adjust the saddle and handlebar still further if you need to, so that your child can sit in the ideal riding position – neither too upright, nor too stretched.

Accessorizing your bike

There are a number of accessories that can be attached to your bike. If you ride during the hours of darkness, you have a legal duty to display a white light at the front and a red light to the rear of your bike.

A range of lights is available to fit any bike, but some accessories, such as bottle cages and child seats, require there to be threaded fixing bosses on the bike's frame. Also, any child carried in a child seat must wear a cycle helmet specifically designed for their age.

Other useful accessories include bike locks, which are essential if you leave your bike in a public place, and saddle bags, which are the best place to store spares, such as a spare inner tube, tyre levers, and a multi-tool.

Child seat

Rear light

Front light

U-lock

Bottle cage

Affixing accessories
Position items so that they do not interfere with one another. The child seat obscures the rear light, so would have to be removed at night.

Lights

There are various attachment methods for lights, but the most popular types clip onto a bracket bolted to the handlebar (front lights) or seat post (rear lights). This means the lights can be easily unclipped so you can take them with you when you leave your bike.

Bottle cage

Cages can be mounted on your bike that are made specifically to carry drinks bottles. This allows you to take a drink on your rides, which helps prevent possible dehydration. There are usually two sets of bosses on bike frames – one set on the downtube and one on the seat tube.

Lock

Bike locks, like this U-lock, are essential for securing your bike in public areas. They can be carried on a mount – usually supplied with the lock when you buy it – that fits on to your bike frame. Follow the manufacturer's fitting instructions and check periodically that the mount is secure. Check for cracks on it too.

Saddle bag

Bags fit under the saddle by means of velcro loops or a mount that is fixed to the saddle rails, as is the case with this one. The bag can then be clipped on and off the mount, or the velcro released. Most bags come with instructions and they must be followed exactly, for ease of use and for safety reasons. Check your bag is securely mounted before each ride.

Child seat

1 **Every child seat** has a mount that fits to your bike, and the seat is then attached to the mount.

● This mount is a pannier rack, which fits a bike that has threaded pannier bosses on its frame. Assemble the mount, then apply grease to the bolts that attach it to the frame.

● Screw the mounting bolts into the pannier bosses, fixing the rack to the frame.

2 **With the rack** securely mounted on your bike, you can attach the seat to it.

● Again, there will be specific instructions supplied with each make and type of seat. Follow them carefully, ensuring that the bolts are tight.

● Fit the child's safety harness, plus the padding and grips provided by the manufacturer for comfort and safety.

3 **Some seats have** an extra fail-safe device. This seat has a safety strap that anchors the seat to the bike's seat post.

● It is a good idea to inspect the seat and its mount, checking every bolt for tightness, after the first ride with a child sitting in it.

● Check the seat and its mount periodically, depending on how often you use it.

Fitting a cycle computer and GPS

Feedback is a great spur to riding, which is why cycle computers are a useful item to have on your bike. Knowing how fast and how far you have travelled, and even how much altitude you have gained – an option on some computers – adds another dimension to your riding.

It's also good to know where you're going – it encourages you to try new routes and explore. GPS devices do just that, as well as many of the things that cycle computers do.

STEP LOCATOR

Parts of a cycle computer and GPS unit

Cycle computer and parts

Sensor

Computer

Magnet

Cadence sensor

GPS unit and parts

GARMIN

GPS unit

Crank magnet

Toolbox

● Small screwdriver or Allen keys (as necessary)
● Cable cutters or scissors (to trim tie wraps)

Fitting a cycle computer

Fit the magnet to a spoke on one of your bike's wheels. The manufacturer's instructions will say which wheel and exactly how to attach it. Magnets come in two varieties: either in two halves that fit around a spoke, or as a unit that clips onto a spoke.

● This magnet fits around a spoke. Open it up (*inset*), put one half on one side of your chosen spoke, then attach the other half to hold it in place.

Fit the computer mount to your handlebar. This mount is secured with tie-wraps, but others may be affixed with a clamp and bolt. Ensure the mount fits securely.

● This is a wireless model, but if your computer has a wire connecting the sensor and mount, tie-wrap it to your fork, then wind it around the front-brake cable-outer until level with the handlebar. Allow enough slack so as not to impede steering.

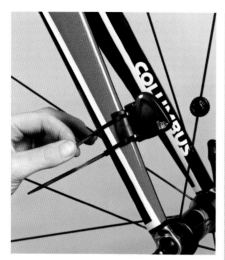

2 **Fit the sensor to your bike.** This one is attached to the fork with tie-wraps. Follow the instructions, and make sure that the correct side of the sensor is facing the spokes.

● Line the sensor up with the magnet. There is often a light indicator on the sensor to show that it has detected the magnet. Turn the wheel to run the magnet past the sensor a few times, then adjust the sensor until the light flashes.

4 **Programme your computer** by following the manufacturer's instructions, then clip it to the handlebar mount.

● If the computer has a heart-rate function, it's worth checking that it works while you are seated on the bike. If it doesn't work, you might have to mount the computer on your bike's stem to bring it within range of the sensor, which you wear on a chest strap.

Fitting a GPS unit

1 **Attach any ancillary devices first.** This GPS unit has a pedal-cadence sensor, which requires a magnet to be fitted to the left-hand crank, then the sensor is tie-wrapped to the left-hand chainstay.

● Check that the sensor and magnet of any ancillary devices line up before continuing.

2 **Fit the GPS mount** to the handlebars or the stem.

● Some mounts are attached with bolted clamps, but this one is secured with an elastic loop.

● Programme the GPS unit, following the instructions that came with it, or the prompts that appear on the screen when switched on. Then clip the unit onto the mount (*inset*).

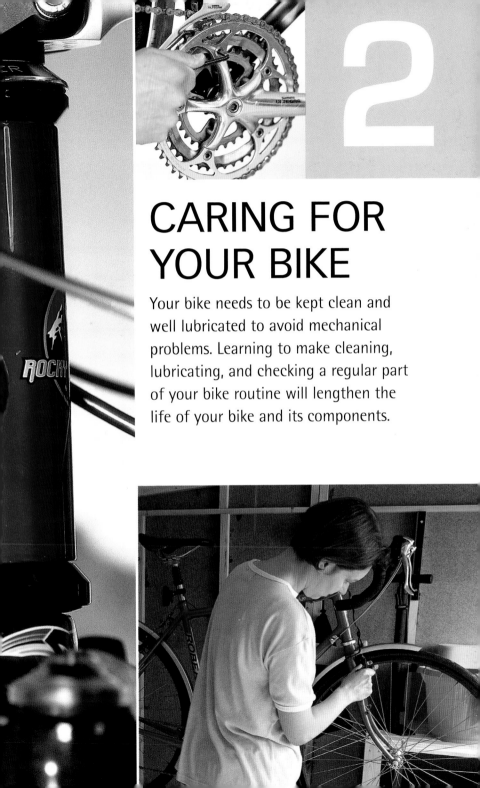

CARING FOR YOUR BIKE

Your bike needs to be kept clean and well lubricated to avoid mechanical problems. Learning to make cleaning, lubricating, and checking a regular part of your bike routine will lengthen the life of your bike and its components.

Tools

If you are going to regularly maintain and repair your bike, you will need to buy a toolkit or assemble your own. The tools shown opposite will enable you to carry out all the essential repairs and to maintain your bike at peak performance. Add other tools as the need arises when specific parts of your bike require maintenance or replacing. However, try to follow a few general principles when using the tools.

When using tools on a bike, especially lightweight bikes, you need a delicate touch. If you are used to working on cars, then use less force when dealing with your bike. Nuts and bolts only need to be tight; if you over-tighten them they will shear. If in doubt, buy torque gauges that accurately measure the correct level of tightness on a bike's nuts and bolts. See the component manufacturers' instructions for recommended torque settings. In fact, it is essential to keep all the instructions that come with your bike, tools, and any components you buy.

Buy the best-quality, precision-made tools. They will last for many years if you look after them. Cheap tools will bend and become chipped, making it impossible to carry out some maintenance jobs properly. They could even damage the components that you work on.

Working with tools
When using your tools to maintain or repair your bike, give yourself plenty of room and always work in a tidy, well-lit environment.

Essential toolkits

Start your toolkit with the two multi-tools, the spanners to fit the cones, long-nosed pliers, cable cutters, a pump, and a workstand.

Pumps and Workstand

Workstand

Frame-fitting pump

Shock pump

Track pump

Spanners and Allen Keys

Spanners 13-18mm

Allen keys 2-10mm

Spanner multi-tool

Allen key multi-tool

Mallet

Plastic mallet

Transmission Tools

Crank-bolt remover

Chain whip

Crank puller

Chain tool

Cassette remover

Bottom Bracket Tools

Peg spanner

Hollow-axle cup tool

Spanner

Hollow-axle crank cap tool

Bottom-bracket remover

Pliers and Cable Cutters

Long-nosed pliers (narrow)

Cable cutters

Long-nosed pliers (wide)

SPECIALIST TOOLS

Some maintenance and replacement tasks require specialist tools that you will not use very often. Other tools, such as the cable puller, are not essential but will make some jobs easier.

Cable puller

Chain measuring device

Bench vice

Spoke keys and spoke ruler

Workshop principles

Four key principles govern the work on your bike. The most useful is tidiness – find a place for each tool and return it there when you have finished with it. Second, do not use too much force to tighten components – the nuts and bolts of lightweight parts can easily shear. Third, remember the order in which you take components apart. Finally, keep all of your tools clean and dry.

The guidelines below provide you with general principles for some of the most common tools or operations in bike repair.

Using Allen keys

Put the long axis of an Allen key in the Allen bolt to make the key easier to use, both for repeated turns and in places where space is tight or restricted, such as putting a bottle cage on the down tube.

Use the short axis of an Allen key to make the final turn when tightening an Allen bolt – for example, on a chainring. You can also use this technique to start undoing an Allen bolt.

Using pliers

Use long-nosed pliers to hold cables and keep them under tension. Buy a small pair with pointed jaws for tight areas. Keep the jaws clean and grease-free. Lubricate the pivot with light oil occasionally.

Fix a cable tidy on to a brake cable to stop the ends from fraying. Push the cable tidy on to the end of the cable and squeeze it flat with your pliers. If you are gentle, you can use the inside jaws of your cable cutters.

Using a spanner

Always use the correct size of spanner for the nut you are tightening or loosening. Hold the spanner firmly at the end to maximize leverage. Make sure that the jaws fully enclose the nut to prevent it from slipping.

Cutting cable outers

Cut a brake cable outer between the spirals of the metal tube under the sheath. If the spirals become compressed, squeeze them with the inside of your cutter jaws until they are round.

Cut a gear cable outer through the wire under the sheath. If you need to, squeeze the wire with the inside of your cutter jaws until its cross-section is round again.

Organizing a bike workshop

Regularly maintaining your bike and carrying out essential repairs means that you can keep your bike at peak performance. If you have the space, the best place to do this is in a workshop that is well organized and equipped with all the tools you need for your particular bike. Create a workshop that is dry with plenty of light – and follow the four key workshop principles.

Cleaning your bike

Although a bike is a very efficient and durable machine, some of its more delicate parts are at the mercy of the elements. Grit and dirt, for example, stick to lubricants and act as a grinding agent. Clean the parts regularly to keep them running smoothly and prevent them from wearing out.

While cleaning your bike, check all the parts and components for damage. With the wheels taken out, you can look at parts of the bike's frame that are usually hidden and examine each component for signs of dangerous wear (see pp.40–1 and pp.46–7).

The process of cleaning is straightforward. First remove old lubricants by applying a degreaser. Then wash the dirt off with water and detergent. Finally, rinse, dry, and lubricate the exposed moving parts.

Cleaning equipment
- Plastic bucket ● Sponges ● Degreaser ● Cloth
- Hard-bristled brushes ● Cassette scraper

Removing dirt and oil

1 **Remove both wheels** from the bike and put the frame in a workstand or hang it up.

● Place a chain holder in the rear drop-out to keep the chain tight while the rear wheel is out of the bike. This allows the chain to run freely so that it can be cleaned thoroughly.

● Apply a degreaser to remove any old oil and grit. Spray on to the chainset, front and rear mechs, and the chain, covering each link.

4 **Clean the rest of the wheel,** including the tyres, with a bigger brush and soapy water.

● Work the bristles in between the spokes and around the hub. Rinse with clean water and dry everything with a cloth.

5 **Spray the chainrings,** chainset, and front mech with more degreaser if there is still stubborn oil and dirt (inset).

● Dip the sponge into hot, soapy water and wrap it around the chain. Turn the pedals so the chain runs through the sponge.

● Use the sponge to wash the rear mech (especially its jockey wheels), the front mech, and chainrings.

2 Use a cassette scraper to gouge out any dirt and debris that has accumulated between the sprockets.

3 Use a hard-bristled brush on the cassette so that the degreaser reaches into the spaces between the sprockets. Allow a few minutes for the degreaser to work and wash off with soapy water.

6 Apply plenty of soapy water to the rest of the bike with a different sponge. Start at the top and work down.

- Use different-sized, hard-bristled brushes to work the water into the places that are hard to reach.

- Rinse with clean water and dry the bike with a clean cloth.

- Use a sponge to work soap into intricate parts, such as between the brake arms and the pads.

- Replace the wheels and sparingly apply a light oil to the chain and the moving parts of the front and rear mechs.

Lubricating your bike

Regular lubrication helps a bike to run smoothly and prevents excessive wear and tear. Each time a part of the bike is lubricated, remember to remove the old oil and grease with degreaser first (*see pp.36–7*). Applying new lubrication on top of old does not work because lubricants attract grit and dirt to the bike and form a grinding paste that can cause damage.

The lubricants needed vary from light spray oil (dry lube) and heavier oil (wet lube) to light grease manufactured specifically for bikes and anti-seize compounds.

STEP LOCATOR

Applying oil and grease

1 **Dribble some light oil** inside the cable outers before you fit a new cable. This makes sure that the cable runs smoothly inside. Poor gear-shifts are often due to cables running dry inside their outers. The same is true of brakes that are hard to apply and slow to return to the ready-to-use position.

3 **Dribble light oil** on to the pivots in the front and rear mechs once a week. The jockey wheels on the rear mech also need some light oil where they rotate around the jockey wheel bolts.

● Make sure that you flush out any old oil with degreaser first.

4 **Oil the chain** after riding in the wet, and clean, dry, and lubricate when cleaning your bike (*see pp.36–7*). Except in winter, or in bad conditions, use light oil from a spray can or bottle.

● Hold a cloth underneath the chain to catch any excess oil.

5 **Grease open bearings** after regular cleaning with a light grease specifically made for bikes. Bottom brackets and hubs need most attention, but headsets need regreasing less often. Riding regularly in the rain shortens the interval between lubrications.

Smear grease on all new cables and, occasionally, on old ones.

● Place a blob of grease on the nipple end of the cable, then pull the cable through your thumb and forefinger before fitting it. Wear mechanic's disposable gloves.

Spread anti-seize compound on the seat pin and stem to prevent the two components from binding with the seat tube or steerer tube. Although you can use grease in place of anti-seize, always use a copper-based anti-seize compound for lubricating components made with carbon fibre.

Making routine safety checks

Every week or so, check the bike frame for signs of wear. Before going for a ride, run through a few checks to reduce the chances of a mechanical failure: brakes that cease to work, a loose handlebar, a tyre blow-out, or slipping gears. The checks will help to avoid many of the accidents caused by equipment failures. Safety checks help the management of a bike, allowing the replacement of parts in good time or the completion of non-urgent maintenance work.

STEP LOCATOR

Making frame checks

1 Inspect the frame every week or so and look for metal fatigue. Run a finger under the down tube where it joins the head tube. A ripple in the tube's surface could lead to a break.

● Check around the area where the chainstay bridge is brazed to the chainstays, particularly on a steel frame. Cracks may form in the metal here because of the heat of the brazing process.

Making pre-ride checks

1 Hold the front wheel firmly between your legs and try to turn the handlebar from one side to the other. If there is any movement, check the stem and steerer bolts and tighten them if necessary.

● Try twisting the bar upwards to look for rotational movement.

2 Apply each brake fully and push the bike forwards. If the lever pulls to the bar before the brake stops a wheel rotating, adjust the travel or replace the pads.

● Apply the front brake. Tighten the headset if you feel any play in the steerer.

3 Lift the bike, slowly spin the wheels, and check the tyres for cuts, splits, or bulges. If you find a bulge, or are in any doubt, replace the tyre. Check the tyre pressure.

● Remove anything stuck in the tyre, as it may cause the tyre to deflate (see pp.116–17).

2 **Monitor all the parts that are riveted to an aluminium frame,** especially the cable guides or the front mech hangers. The rivets form potentially weak areas where stresses in the metal may develop into cracks.

3 **Protect carbon-fibre frames** in areas where the cable outers touch them. Buy a self-adhesive protective patch and peel off the back. Place it on the frame, sticky side down, under the cable outer – it is very important to prevent the cable from wearing down the carbon frame. Check the patches regularly and replace them when worn.

4 **Check that all quick-release** levers are in the locked position, and wheel nuts are tight. Look for the words "lock" and "unlock" on the levers – "lock" is outermost when the wheel is secure (see pp.114–15).

5 **Run through the gears** and make sure that they are properly adjusted. Gears that will not mesh properly after you change them can be distracting and, if you look down to see what is wrong, potentially dangerous. If the gears are correctly adjusted and the chain is still jumping, check for a stiff link.

Servicing

Schedule the work you need to carry out on your bike by developing a servicing timetable. The timetable on the right provides a good template since it shows the tasks you should perform on your bike and suggests when you should do them.

Your schedule depends on how much and where your bike is ridden. A heavily-used, off-road bike requires attention at much shorter intervals than a bike used for infrequent, short road journeys.

However, work carried out as part of a service schedule does not replace the safety checks that must be carried out before every ride (see pp.40–1), or regularly looking for danger signs (see pp.46–7). You should also check your bike and lubricate the transmission every time you clean it.

SERVICING TIMETABLE

EVERY WEEK

TRANSMISSION	CHECK	Chain for wear (see pp.72–5). Gear-shift performance (see pp.54–9, 62–5). Inner cables for fraying and outer cables for wear (see pp.46–7, 54–9). Cranks and chainring bolts for tightness (see pp.78–
	LUBRICATE	Oil chain (see pp.38–9). Oil jockey wheels (see pp.64–5).
	REPLACE	
STEERING AND WHEELS	CHECK	Headset for looseness and ease of steering (see pp.100–3). Action of quick-release levers (see pp.114–15). Wheels for broken spokes and trueness (see pp.119– Handlebar and stem for cracks (see pp.104–7).
	LUBRICATE	
	REPLACE	
BRAKES	CHECK	Inner cables for fraying and and outer cables for we (see pp.46–7, 124–7). Pads for wear and alignment (see pp.128–35, 140– Hydraulic hoses for wear, kinks, or leaks (see pp.47, 142–3). Brake levers, arms, discs, and callipers for cracks (see pp.124–35, 140–3). Disc and calliper bolts for tightness (see pp.142–3).
	LUBRICATE	Oil-exposed cables by wiping with wet lube on a ra
	REPLACE	
SUSPENSION	CHECK	Fork and shock exterior surfaces for cracks (see pp.154–7, 164–5). Stanchions under shock boots, if fitted, for cracks (see pp.152–3). Top caps, crown bolts, and shaft bolts for tightness (see pp.150–1, 154–7).
	LUBRICATE	Teflon oil on fork stanchions and shock body, and on all seals (see pp.160–1, 166–7).
	REPLACE	

EVERY MONTH

Bottom bracket for smooth running, play, and bent axle (see pp.82-7).
Pedals for play, and clipless pedals for play and release action (see pp.90-3).
Rear mech pivots for play (see pp.64-5).
Sprocket and chainring teeth for wear (see pp.76-7).

Oil mech pivots (see pp.38-9).
Oil and grease inner and outer cables (see pp.38-9).
Oil clipless pedal release mechanisms (see pp.48-9).

Chain on a heavily used bike (see pp.72-5).

Hubs for play on axles, roughness, or tight spots (see pp.112-13).
Rubber seals on hubs for splits (see pp.112-13).
Covers, if fitted, on headsets (see pp.48-9).

Oil the seals on hubs (see pp.112-13).

Discs for wear and callipers for alignment (see pp.144-5).

Grease inner cables and oil inside outer cables (see pp.38-9, 124-7).

Brake pads of heavily used mountain bikes (see pp.130-3, 138-9).

Fork and shock for play (see pp.152-7, 164-5).
Fork stanchions to see if oil line visible (see pp.152-7).
Fork and shock seals for cracks and slackness (see pp.152-7, 162-3).
Play, absence of oil lines, and cracked seals are all evidence of worn seals, which should be replaced by a qualified technician.
Fork and shock sag (see pp.152-3, 162-3).

Tip bike upside down and store overnight so oil can redistribute in fork. Clean air filter and lubricate fork leg.

EVERY SIX MONTHS

Freehub body and freewheel for play (see pp.76-7).
Rear mech frame fixing bolt for play (see pp.64-5).
Cleats for wear (see pp.94-5).
Jockey wheels for wear (see pp.64-5).

Oil in hub gear, if equipped with oil port (see pp.68-9).
Grease bearings in pedals (see pp.90-1).

Chain (see pp.72-5).
Inner and outer cables (see pp.54-9).
Sprockets on a heavily used bike (see pp.76-7).

Bearings in open-bearing hubs for wear (see pp.112-13).
Bearings and bearing surfaces in headsets for wear (see pp.100-3).

Grease open-bearing hubs (see pp.112-13).
Grease headsets (see pp.100-3).

Handlebar tape and grips (see pp.104-7).

Grease brake bosses (see pp.130-3).

Inner and outer cables (see pp.124-7).

Fork steerer for cracks, by removing the headset (see pp.100-3).

Check bushings and bearings in rear suspension for play, and lubricate them.

Fork oil (see pp.154-7).
Seals on forks and shocks, as part of bi-annual service by qualified technician.

Troubleshooting

The symptoms of some of the things that can go wrong with your bike are listed in this troubleshooting chart. It explains why a bike may be showing these symptoms and then suggests a solution, referring you to the pages where you will find a detailed sequence of steps to guide you.

If you still find the problem difficult to solve, consult the How They Work pages for the specific part you are working on, so that you can understand it better. However, sometimes, the symptoms confronting you can be due to a different malfunction to the one suggested in this chart. If after consulting the relevant pages in the book you still cannot solve the problem, ask the experts at a good bike shop for help.

SOLVING COMMON PROBLEM

PROBLEM

TRANSMISSION

The chain will not shift on to a smaller sprocket or chainring.

The chain will not shift on to a larger sprocket or it shift but does not run smoothly on it.

The chain shifts cleanly, but jumps on the sprockets when pressure is applied to the pedals.

The chain rubs on the inner then the outer side of the front mech cage. On a bike with a single chainring, the chain persistently falls off.

STEERING AND WHEELS

When you apply the front brake and push the bike forwards, the headset moves forwards relative to the head tube.

You hear a sudden snapping noise come from a wheel while riding and/or the wheel goes out of true.

There is side-to-side play of a hub on its axle, or when turning the axle in the hub you feel either a roughness or tight and loose spots.

When pedalling forwards, the cassette spins, but there is no drive to the bike. Alternatively, the cassette spins before the drive is engaged or there is much side-to-side play in the cassette.

BRAKES

The brakes are hard to apply, and/or sluggish to release.

You have to pull the brake lever a long way before the brakes engage.

The two brake pads do not contact the braking surface a the same time.

The brake pads contact the braking surface without pulli the lever too far, but are ineffective at slowing the bike.

SUSPENSION

The fork regularly reaches the limit of its travel (bottoms c

On steep, smooth descents, the rear wheel lifts under braking.

The front wheel judders up and down when cornering.

A rear air/oil shock regularly reaches the limit of its trav (bottoms out).

CAUSE	SOLUTION
Either grit has become lodged inside the cable outers or the cable lubrication has dried up.	Strip down the cables, flush the outers with degreaser, clean the inners with degreaser, lubricate, and reassemble (see pp.38-9, 54-9).
The cable has stretched or the relevant mech is poorly adjusted.	Unclamp the cable at the mech, pull through any slack, and re-tighten. Then set up the mech (see pp.62-5).
Either the chain has a stiff link; or the chain or sprockets, or both, are worn; or a chainring may be bent.	Check the chain for a stiff link and remove it if found. If no stiff link, replace the chain. If the problem persists, replace the sprockets. If the chainring is bent, replace it (see pp.72-9).
The bottom bracket is worn or its axle may be bent.	If the bottom bracket is a cartridge type, replace it. If it is a hollow-axle bottom bracket, replace the cup and bearing units. If it is a press-fit bottom bracket, it may be possible to replace the bearings if they are worn (see pp.82-7).
The headset is loose or worn.	Strip and inspect the headset. Replace bearings if worn, regrease, and reassemble. Inspect the cups and races; if they are worn you should let a good bike shop replace the whole headset (see pp.100-3).
A spoke may have broken.	Replace the spoke and true the wheel (see pp.118-19).
The hub bearings are worn or, in the case of tight and loose spots, the axle is bent.	Replace the bearings or the axle (see pp.112-13).
The freehub body is worn.	Replace the freehub body (see pp.76-7, 112-13).
Grit and dirt is inside the cable outers or the lubrication on the inner cables has dried.	Strip down the cables, flush the outers, and clean the inner cables with degreaser, lubricate both, and reassemble (see pp.38-9, 124-7).
The pads are wearing down or the cable has slipped through the clamp bolt.	If the pads are not too worn, take up the extra travel by unclamping the brakes, pulling the cable through the clamp, and tightening. If the pads are worn, replace them (see pp.122-35, 138-47).
Your brakes are not centred.	Follow the procedures for centring the type of brakes on your bike (see pp.122-35, 138-47).
There is grease on the pads, foreign bodies embedded in them, or they are wearing unevenly. You may even need a different compound of brake pad.	Rub the pads with emery cloth. Remove foreign bodies with long-nosed pliers. Fit new pads if they are worn unevenly. Seek advice from a bike shop regarding different pad compounds (see pp.122-35, 138-47).
With air/oil forks, not enough air is in the system. With coil/oil forks, too light a spring is fitted.	Pump in more air. Replace springs with heavier duty springs (see pp.152-5).
The front of the bike is diving under braking because the fork is not stiff enough.	Pump in air, or increase pre-load, according to the type of fork on your bike (see pp.152-5).
The fork's rebound is set too fast.	Use the relevant adjuster to reduce the speed of the fork's rebound (see pp.152-5).
Insufficient air in the shock, or too much damping, means that the shock is not returning from each compression quickly enough.	Set up the sag on the shock again. If the problem continues, use the damping adjustment to speed up the action of the shock (see pp.164-5).

Spotting danger signs

The more you ride your bike, the quicker the various moving parts, particularly tyres and brake pads, will wear away. Replacing the parts as soon as they become worn not only keeps the bike running smoothly but also reduces the chances of an accident. You will save money, too, since worn parts have the knock-on effect of wearing out other parts.

As you run through your safety checks (see pp.40–1), look for worn teeth on sprockets and chainrings, worn brake pads, split or frayed cables, worn wheel rims, bulging or split tyres, and worn tyre treads. If you spot any danger signs, take action as soon as you can. You must replace a damaged part before you next ride your bike.

Checking for wear
Regularly check the tyres, rims, brakes, chainrings, cables, and sprockets so that you can spot signs of wear as early as possible.

Cables and hoses

Rims and tyres

Brakes

Sprockets

Chainrings

Sprockets and chainrings
Worn teeth

Regularly check for worn or missing teeth on a chainring or sprocket. The chain can jump when you apply pressure to the pedals, especially if you are out of the saddle, and you may be pitched forwards and crash. Replace the chainring or sprocket as soon as you see this sign (see pp.76–9).

Brakes
Worn brake pads

Regularly check all the brake pads for uneven wear. This is a sign that they are not contacting the braking surface evenly. The effectiveness of your brakes is compromised, because not all the pad's surface is in use. Fit new pads and adjust your brakes correctly (see pp.128–35).

Rims and tyres

Look for evidence of deep scoring on the rims of each of your bike's wheels. Rim brakes will gradually wear out the rims, especially if you ride off-road or in winter. Eventually, the rims will fail and you could crash. Cracks around the nipples of the spokes where they join the rim are a danger sign, too. Replace the rim if you see these signs.

Worn rim

Split or bulging tyre

Worn tread

Check the whole circumference of the tyres on both wheels for bulges or splits in the tread or walls. Tyres with bulges, distortions, or splits anywhere on them are likely to blow when you ride your bike. If you spot any of these failures on your tyre, replace it immediately (*see pp.116–17* for how to remove and refit a tyre).

Look closely at the tread of both tyres for signs of wear. If the tread is worn, the tyre has lost structural strength and can break down and distort or bulge. The result can be a blow-out during the course of a single ride. A tyre that has been skidded and lost enough rubber to develop a flat spot can also be dangerous. Replace the tyre if you see either sign (*see pp.116–17*).

Cables and hoses
Split or leaking hose

Split or frayed cables

Split brake outer

Frayed gear outer

Check the entire length of each brake hose – fitted on bikes with hydraulic brakes to carry fluid from the brake lever to the brake itself – for splits or any sign of leaking brake fluid. The evidence might be as little as a single droplet or a smear of fluid. Leakages need immediate attention from a qualified mechanic, who will be able to replace the brake hose with a new one.

Check all cables and cable outers for signs of splitting and fraying. Frayed inner cables can snap, leaving you without gears, which is inconvenient, or without brakes, which is dangerous. Change the cable before you ride again (*see pp.54–9, 124–7*). Worn or split outers reduce the effectiveness of your brakes and allow dirt to get in and clog the cables. Change the outer as soon as you can.

Preparing for wet weather

These steps will help you to prepare a bike for the rigours of winter, a particularly wet climate, or if most of your riding is done off-road. The mud, sand, and water that your wheels spray up into every part of the bike combine to form a damaging, grinding paste. Salt, often used to treat roads where ice is likely to occur, will quickly corrode your bike. Regular cleaning and lubricating helps with protection, but try to stop the mud and salt from reaching the delicate parts of the bike in the first place. The overall aim when protecting a bike in winter is to prevent water reaching non-exposed parts and stop water from washing off the lubricant on exposed parts.

Protecting a bike
Fit mudguards, insert seals, and lubricate the exposed parts to protect a bike from wet conditions.

Mudguard

Headset

Mech

Seat post collar

Pedal

Chain

Shielding exposed components

Sealing the seat post collar

Keep water out of the point where the seat pin enters the frame. Mark this junction and remove the pin. Pull a piece of narrow road bike inner tube over the frame. Insert the pin through the tube to the mark and tie-wrap the tube to secure it.

Sealing the headset

Place a cover over the headset to provide protection. You can fit a protector to the headset without removing any components by simply joining up the velcro.

Fitting mudguards

Fasten a mudguard to the seat pin and you will block much of the spray from the back wheel. For the front wheel, fit a guard that clips on to the frame and is secured in place with tie-wraps. Full mudguards, which attach to the fork and rear drop-out, give almost full protection for on-road biking but get clogged up off-road.

Weatherproofing the transmission

Cleaning and lubricating the chain

Lubricate and clean your chain as often as you do in summer and after every wet ride. Apply the same light lubricant that you use in the summer and then apply a heavier oil, which will not wash off as easily. Only coat the rollers and insides of each link with heavier oil because it attracts more dirt.

Cleaning and lubricating mechs

Dribble oil on to the pivots around which the front and rear mechs move. Use a heavier, wet oil rather than the oil you would normally apply during the summer. Every time you dribble oil like this, first flush out the old oil by dribbling some degreaser on to the pivots and letting it sink in for a few minutes.

Cleaning and lubricating pedals

Apply heavier, wet oil to lubricate the retention mechanism of clipless pedals after degreasing all the moving parts. The heavier oil will not wash off as easily as dry oil. Regularly clean off old oil with degreaser and apply new oil in order to prevent the accumulation of grit and the consequent increase in pedal wear.

MAINTAINING YOUR TRANSMISSION

The transmission is the heart of your bike. Fine-tune and regularly service the system to ensure that the gear-shifters, chain, chainset, cassette, and mechs work together in perfect harmony.

CABLES AND SHIFTERS

Cables and shifters enable the rider to operate the gears. Cables are under constant tension and need to be replaced regularly and kept well lubricated. They must also be inspected often and replaced if they show signs of wear. Shifters require only occasional lubrication of their inner workings.

How they work

An inner cable connects the gear-shifter to the mech, and allows the rider to change gear. Gear-shifts made by a gear-shifter cause the front mech to shift the chain from one chainring to another, or the rear mech to shift the chain from one sprocket to another. Pulling the gear cable shifts the chain from a smaller to a larger chainring or sprocket; releasing the gear cable shifts the chain from a larger to a smaller chainring or sprocket. The left-hand shifter controls the front mech; the right-hand shifter controls the rear mech.

Controlling the gears
The cables and shifters on a bike allow the rider to effortlessly control the gear system.

Cable clamp
Attaches the cable to the rear mech

Rear mech
Moves the chain from one sprocket to another

REAR MECH CABLE

A clamp connects the cable to the rear mech. When the shifter is pushed, the cable pulls the rear mech inwards, moving the chain from a smaller to a larger sprocket. When the shifter releases the cable tension, the springs on the rear mech pull the jockey wheels, and the chain, back to a smaller sprocket.

Front mech
Moves the chain from one chainring to another

SHIFTING GEAR

In this Campagnolo shifter, the rider pushes the inner shift lever to pull the cable and move the mech. When the rider depresses a lever on the inner side of the lever hood, the cable is released and the mech moves back.

Gear-shifter
Pulls and releases the gear cable

COMBINED BRAKE LEVER/GEAR-SHIFTER ANATOMY

Gear-shifters are often combined with the brake levers on the handlebar. On this Shimano gear-shifter, the brake lever also acts as a shift lever. When the rider pushes the brake lever inwards with the fingers, the control cable attached to it is pulled and a ratchet mechanism is lifted. A click of this mechanism equals one shift of the front or rear mech, which moves the chain across the chainring or sprockets. The ratchet mechanism then holds the cable in its new position. When the rider pushes the inner shift lever inwards, the ratchet mechanism's hold is released and so the shifter's pull on the cable ceases.

Cable
Connects the shifter to the rear mech

Lever hood
Attaches the levers to the handlebar

Ratchet mechanism
Holds the cable

Cable inner
Controls a mech

Inner shift lever
Releases the cable

Cable outer
Counteracts the cable pull

Brake lever
Pulls the cable

Drop handlebar gear cable

Keeping your bike's gear cables clean and lubricated – and replacing them if they fray – is important for smooth shifting. Change them at least once a year, or more often if you are a heavy user.

Lubrication reduces the effects of friction between the inner cable and the cable outer, and helps to keep out water and grit. If the gears become difficult to shift to a different chainring or sprocket, the cable is probably dry and needs lubrication.

These steps show how to fit a new gear cable to a SRAM shifter. Fitting cables to gear shifters made by other manufacturers, such as Shimano and Campagnolo, will be slightly different, but the order of each task in the overall sequence is broadly the same.

STEP LOCATOR

Parts of gear-shift units

SRAM shifter

Rubber brake hood cover

Shimano shifter

Brake lever

Gear-shift lever

Brake lever

Gear-shift lever

Toolbox

- Allen key multi-tool • Long-nosed pliers
- Cable cutters • Oil

Replacing a SRAM gear cable

1 **Use the shifter to move the chain** to the smallest sprocket if you are fitting a new rear-mech gear cable, or to the smallest chainring for a new front-mech gear cable.

● To do this with Shimano and SRAM shifters, move the inner shift lever towards the centre line of the bike.

● To do this with Campagnolo shifters, push down on the lever situated on the inner side of the lever hoods.

4 **Push the new, lubricated cable** into the same hole that you removed the old cable from. When the end emerges behind the lever hood, pull until the nipple fits snugly in place.

● For a Shimano shifter (*inset*), pull the brake lever to reveal the the cable insertion point, which is located beneath the hood cover on the outside of the lever. Feed the cable through the shifter and pull on it until the nipple sits in place.

Undo the cable clamp bolt on the mech, then release the old cable and push it through the guidance boss on the mech.

● Note the path by which the cable enters the mech and how it sits in the cable clamp. You must replicate this with the new cable.

● If the cable is frayed, cut off the frayed end with a pair of cable cutters, to allow it to pass through the guidance boss and the outer cables.

Remove the old cable from a SRAM or Campagnolo shifter by rolling the rubber lever-hood cover forwards.

● Push the cable from behind the shifter and watch where the cable nipple emerges from the side of the shifter hood body (*inset*).

● For Shimano shifters, the cable emerges from under the hood cover without rolling it forwards.

● Pull the old cable from the shifter by its nipple.

Dribble a little oil into the cable outers and insert the cable through the outers. Make sure they are firmly seated in the cable guides on the frame. If you are fitting new outers, cut them to the same length as the ones they replace.

● Ensure metal ferrules are fitted to both ends of each outer.

Pull the cable through all the outers and cable guides, and reconnect it to the mech by tightening the cable clamp bolt.

● Re-fasten the cable so that it is in exactly the same position as it was when you unfastened the clamp bolt in Step 2.

● Ensure that you pull the cable tight through the clamp bolt before you fasten it.

Bar-end gear cable

Triathlon and time-trial bikes are equipped with bar-end shifters, which are located on the ends of the tri-bar extensions. Tri-bars allow cyclists to adopt a low, aerodynamic riding position, while bar-end shifters make changing gear possible without the need to alter that position.

Bar-end shifters must be well maintained, since the shifters are further from the front or rear mech than on any other type of bike, apart from a tandem. Fitting new cables must also be done with care and precision. The cable outers should be short enough to allow the cables to follow as straight a line as possible, without restricting steering.

STEP LOCATOR

Parts of a bar-end gear-shift unit

Shift lever

Expanding joint

Shifter body

Tension adjuster

Lever cover

Toolbox
- Allen key multi-tool • Long-nosed pliers
- Cable cutters • Oil

Replacing a bar-end gear cable

1 **Shift the chain** onto the smallest sprocket or chainring, then unclamp the cable from the front or rear mech cable, depending on which cable you are replacing.

- Pull the gear-shift lever back, then push it forwards to expose the cable and its nipple.

- If the cable nipple doesn't come out of the shifter, remove any handlebar tape from the tri-bar extensions – it might be restricting the cable.

4 **Thread the cable** through the mech and its clamp bolt.

- While pulling the end of the cable to preserve tension in it, tighten the clamp bolt with a 5mm Allen key.

- Trim the gear cable with your cable cutters, leaving around 1cm (³⁄₈in) on the outside of the cable-clamp bolt.

Pull the old cable out of the shifter by the cable nipple.

- Grab the nipple with long-nosed pliers and pull it to get it started. Once there is enough cable to hold with your fingers, it should come all the way out by pulling.

Ensure the shift lever is pushed back all the way into the smallest sprocket or chainring position.

- Insert the new gear cable into the shifter at the same point where the old one came out.

- Push the cable through the shifter and first length of cable outer, then pull the end, feeding it through any further outers until it reaches the front or rear mech.

Crimp a cable tidy onto the end of the new cable (*inset*). If cable ends are left uncovered they can fray and look untidy – a cable tidy will prevent that.

- Place the tidy over the cable end and use the inside edge of your cable cutters to squeeze it in place.

- Some cable cutters have notches on their inside edges to make the job easier, but the trick is to apply just enough pressure to squeeze the soft metal down onto the cable.

Straight handlebar gear cables

Looking after and replacing the gear cables on a mountain bike is very similar to a road bike. However, mountain bikes are often subjected to harsher conditions than road bikes, as they are often ridden through dirt and mud, so the cables must be replaced and lubricated more regularly.

There are three main kinds of straight handlebar shifter: the Shimano Rapidfire, the Shimano Dual Control, and the SRAM. Replacing a gear cable is similar for them all.

STEP LOCATOR

Parts of gear-shift units

Gear-shift levers
SRAM shifter
Shifter cover
Barrel adjuster
Star nut
Gear-shift levers
Ring clamp
Shimano Rapidfire
Shifter body

Gear-shift lever
Handlebar clamp
Shimano Dual Control
Cable port
Brake lever body
Shifter body
Brake/gear-shift lever

Toolbox

- 5mm Allen key • Long-nosed pliers
- Cable cutters • Cable pullers • Tweezers

Replacing a Rapidfire gear cable

1 **Remove the cable–port cover** with a screwdriver (inset). Put the shifter in the smallest sprocket or chainring position.

- Unclamp the cable–clamp bolt on the mech, then pull the cable housing away from the barrel adjuster on the shifter. Push the inner gear cable out of the shifter so that the nipple emerges.

- Check the route of your existing cable and follow the route when fitting a new cable in Step 4.

3 **Cut both the cable** and cable outers with your cable cutters to the same length as the old ones you have removed. Make the outers long enough to allow the cable to travel freely inside.

- Dribble a drop of oil down each cable outer.

- Fit a ferrule to the end of each cable outer to ensure that it fits tightly into the frame's cable guides (see pp.34–5).

Replacing a SRAM gear cable

2 **Insert the end of the new,** lubricated cable into the hole where the cable nipple sits inside the shifter.

● Push the cable into the hole until its end shows through the barrel adjuster on the outside of the shifter body.

● Thread the cable through the first length of lubricated cable outer.

1 **For the rear cable,** put the shifter into the smallest sprocket. For the front cable, put the front shifter into the smallest chainring. Remove the old cable from the mech, then undo the star nut that holds the shifter cover in place.

● Grab the cable nipple with tweezers and remove it. Insert a new one through the barrel adjuster and seat the nipple into position. Pass the cable through the outers and re-attach it to the mech.

Replacing a Dual Control gear cable

4 **Thread the inner cable** through each length of outer cable.

● For a rear mech, unscrew the barrel adjuster to about half its range and insert the inner cable. For a front mech, insert the cable into the clamp.

● Pull hard with your cable pullers and tighten the cable clamp. Cut off any excess cable.

1 **For the rear cable,** put the shifter into the smallest sprocket. For the front cable, put the front shifter into the smallest chainring.

● Open the cable port to reveal the old cable inside the shifter, and remove it with long-nosed pliers.

● Push the cable into the cable port until the cable nipple sits in the cradle inside the body.

● Follow Step 4 of Replacing a Rapidfire gear cable.

FRONT AND REAR MECHS

The two mechs move the chain smoothly between the sprockets and chainrings, but only if the travel of the mechs is set up correctly. The mech pivots and jockey wheels must be checked for wear and lubricated. The front mech must be properly aligned with the chainrings.

How they work

The front and rear mechs change the gears on a bike. To change up a gear, the shifter is used to pull on the cable, which causes the front mech to push the chain from a smaller to a larger chainring or the rear mech to push the chain from a smaller to a larger sprocket. To change down a gear, the cable is released, causing the springs in both mechs to move the chain to a smaller chainring or sprocket. Each mech moves around a pivot point. High and low adjusting screws ensure that the mechs do not push the chain beyond the largest chainring or sprocket, or pull it beyond the smallest. This range is called the mech's travel. Once its travel is set up, and provided the cable tension is sufficient, the mech will make a single, clean gear-shift for every click of the shifter.

Rear mech
Transfers the chain from one sprocket to another

Cable
Pushes and pulls the rear mech

REAR MECH ANATOMY

To change gear, two jockey wheels transfer the chain on to a different sprocket. They move in the same plane as the chain and are spring-loaded to preserve the tension in the chain. Two mech plates enable the jockey wheels to change gear upwards, while the plate spring enables the jockey wheels to change gear downwards.

Mech plate
Transfers cable pull to the jockey wheels

Plate spring
Pulls the mech back as cable is released

High and low adjusters
Limit the travel of the mech

Jockey wheel spring
Preserves the tension in the chain

Cable clamp
Attaches the cable to the mech plates

Jockey wheel
Pulls and pushes the chain

Cable
Pulls the mech plates

Jockey wheel cage
Holds the jockey wheels

Working with the shifters
The front and rear mechs work in harmony with the shifters to provide easy, quick, and accurate gear-shifts whenever the rider needs them.

REAR MECH IN USE

When the cable is pulled, it causes both the mech plates to swing inwards on four pivot points, causing the jockey wheels to guide the chain on to a larger sprocket. When the cable is released, the plate spring moves the chain back to a smaller sprocket.

Large sprocket *The chain is moved to the largest sprocket by the pull of the cable.*

Small sprocket *The chain is returned to the smallest sprocket by the plate spring.*

FRONT MECH ANATOMY

When pulled, the cable moves the outer arm, which acts like a lever on a pivot point to push the front mech cage away from the bike. This moves the chain from a smaller to a larger chainring. When the cable is released, a spring on the mech's inner arm pulls the cage back towards the bike.

High and low adjusters
Limit the travel of the mech cage

Clamp bolt
Fixes the mech to the frame

Outer arm
Acts as a lever

Cable clamp
Holds the cable to the mech

Pivot point
Acts as a fulcrum for the arm

Mech cage
Moves the chain

Chainring
Engages the chain

Chainring
Carries the chain

Front mech
Transfers the chain from one chainring to another

Front mech

Front mechs (short for "mechanism") shift the chain from one chainring to the next. There are two main kinds: braze-on mechs (below) are fixed by an Allen bolt to a lug, or protrusion, on the bike frame; band-on mechs are attached to a band that goes around the frame and is part of the mech.

There are two important maintenance jobs for a front mech: setting it up after fitting a new control cable and adjusting it when it is not shifting properly. You should also clean the mech regularly to prevent the build-up of dirt, which interferes with the way it works and will quickly wear it out.

For the mech to work perfectly, the lower edge of the mech cage's outer side should be no higher than 2mm above the largest chainring. The cage's outer side must also be parallel with the chainrings.

Correct shifts depend on the front mech travelling a certain distance per shift. High and low adjusting screws on the mech will control this travel.

STEP LOCATOR

Parts of a braze-on front mech

Cable-fixing clamp
Pivots
High/low adjusters
Front mech cage (outer side)
Frame-fixing clamp
Front mech cage (inner side)

Toolbox

- Long-nosed pliers • 5mm Allen key
- Screwdriver • Cable cutters

Adjusting a front mech

1 **Shift the chain** into the largest sprocket and the smallest chainring.

• Pull the front mech cage away from the frame. Note the distance by which the lower edge of its outer side clears the largest chainring. This should be 2mm. If it is more or less, undo the frame-fixing clamp and raise or lower the front mech.

• Line up the cage parallel with the chainrings and tighten the frame-fixing clamp.

3 **Pull the gear cable** through the cable clamp and tighten the cable-clamp bolt.

• Cut off any excess cable with your cable cutters and crimp on a cable tidy (see pp.34–5).

• Repeat Steps 2 and 3 if, after a couple of rides, the chain will not shift up to the next chainring, since cables can sometimes stretch slightly.

2 **Undo the cable-fixing** clamp until the cable becomes free.

● Look for the low gear adjuster (usually marked "L") and screw it in or out until the inner side of the front mech cage is about 2mm from the chain. You have now set the starting point of the mech's travel.

● Take this opportunity to clean the guide in which the cable runs under the bottom-bracket shell. Use degreaser, and then wash and dry the whole area.

● Put a little dry lubricant in the guide.

4 **Shift the chain** across until it is in the smallest sprocket and the largest chainring.

● Repeat Steps 2 and 3 if the chain will not shift on to the largest chainring.

5 **Screw in the high adjuster** (usually marked "H") to bring the outer side of the front mech cage to about 2mm from the chain.

● Unscrew the higher adjuster to allow more travel if, when you shift on to the largest chainring, the chain does not move on to it.

● Check the action by shifting a few times between all the chainrings.

Rear mech

Most rear mechs are indexed, which means that for every click of the shifter, either up or down, the mech will shift the chain from one sprocket to the next.

Occasionally, you may find that the chain does not quite move on to the next sprocket when you make a single shift, or else it skips a sprocket in an overshift. In either case, the rear mech needs adjusting. You will also need to follow the steps in this sequence whenever you fit a new cable (see pp.52–9).

To ensure that the rear mech works faultlessly, pay particular attention to its jockey wheels because this is where oil and dirt can accumulate. Degrease and scrub them every time you clean your bike (see pp.36–7). Whenever you lubricate the jockey wheels or the rear mech pivots, make sure that you wipe off any excess oil.

STEP LOCATOR

Parts of a rear mech

Barrel adjuster

Jockey wheel

Mech pivot

Cable-fixing clamp

Jockey cage

Toolbox

- Long-nosed pliers • Cable cutters
- 5mm Allen key • Screwdriver

Adjusting a rear mech

1 **Shift the chain** on to the biggest chainring and smallest sprocket, then undo the cable-fixing clamp so that the cable hangs free.

- Check the cable and fit a new one if it shows any sign of fraying.

- Screw the barrel adjuster in or out, until it is at half of its range.

4 **Shift back to the smallest sprocket,** then shift upwards through each gear. If the rear mech does not shift all the way on to the next biggest sprocket, screw out the barrel adjuster until it does. If the mech over-shifts and skips a sprocket, screw in the barrel adjuster until it stops.

2 **Use the high** adjuster (usually marked "H") to line up the jockey wheels with the smallest sprocket.

● Once you have lined them up, rotate the pedals forwards while adjusting the "H" adjuster until the chain runs smoothly.

● Pull the cable downwards through the cable-fixing clamp and re-clamp it.

3 **Shift on to the smallest chainring** and largest sprocket.

● Push the rear mech with your fingers towards the spokes. If it moves beyond the largest sprocket, screw in the low adjuster (marked "L") until the mech stops at the largest sprocket.

● Turn the pedals to see if the chain runs smoothly. If it does not, adjust the "L" in or out.

5 **Prevent the jockey wheels** from making contact with the bigger sprockets by screwing in the adjuster that butts on to the rear mech hanger on the frame drop-out. Remember to make this adjustment if you fit a block or cassette with bigger sprockets than usual.

HUB GEARS

Hub gears located inside the hub casing alter the speed at which the back wheel revolves. They require little routine maintenance and, since they are sealed, most hub-gear systems do not need to be lubricated regularly. The control cables must still be inspected regularly and replaced if they are worn.

How they work

All hub gears work according to the same basic principle. A system of internal cogs make the hub casing, and therefore the rear wheel, turn at a different speed to a single, external sprocket that is driven by the pedals via the chain. The sprocket is connected to the cogs by a driver unit and the cogs rotate the hub casing at different speeds. Spokes attach the casing to the rim, thereby revolving the rear wheel.

A shifter on the handlebar operates a mechanism attached to the hub. This mechanism causes various combinations of different-sized cogs within the hub to engage with a ring gear, which drives the hub casing. Each combination gives a different gear ratio, and the number of gears depends on the number of cogs within the hub.

SHIMANO HUB GEAR ANATOMY

To change gear, the rider activates the shifter to pull the cable, which turns the satellite on the drive side of the hub. This triggers a mechanism within the driver unit to move two carrier units containing cogs. Different cogs are brought into contact with the ring gears. When the cable is released, the spring-loaded carrier units move the cogs back to a different combination.

Hub casing
Turns the wheel

Cable and satellite
Side view of the hub

Bearings
Aid the rotation of the hub casing

Driver unit
Transfers the sprocket's drive and causes the carrier unit to engage different cogs with the ring gear

Carrier unit
Carries the different-sized cogs

Ring gear
Turns the hub casing

Protecting the gears
The hub gear mechanism is fully
enclosed to protect it from
damage, dirt, and water.

Hub gear unit
*Contains the cogs that
allow gear changes*

Hub gear

If the cable to your hub gear snaps or shows any signs of wear, you must replace it. Although there are several different makes and models of hub gear, all with subtle differences in the way they work, replacing a gear cable is usually similar to the method pictured here on a Shimano Alfine. The main difference between them is the way the cable couples with the shift mechanism, but each have some form of connector that requires loosening, like the cable-clamp bolt pictured here.

Removing a hub-gear wheel is necessary for fitting a new tyre or mending a puncture, and requires a different procedure to that for bikes with derailleur gears. The other main maintenance demand is regular lubrication – most hub gears have an oil port through which oil can be dribbled.

STEP LOCATOR

Parts of a hub gear

Sprocket

Cable outer

Gear satellite

Cable-clamp bolt

Cable-joint stopper

Toolbox
- Spanners to fit cable-clamp bolt and wheel-axle nuts • Measuring tape

Replacing a hub-gear cable

1 **Click the gear-shifter** so that the chain moves into first gear. This is to remove tension from the gear cable.

- The cable operates a mechanism on the hub called the satellite, which initiates each gear change. Take hold of the satellite and twist it anticlockwise (*inset*).

3 **Measure the distance** from the cable-clamp bolt to the last length of cable outer. You will need this measurement for Step 4.

- Place a spanner on either side of the cable-clamp bolt, then loosen the bolt. Remove the bolt from the old cable.

- Push the old cable through any other lengths of cable outer, then remove it from the shifter.

Removing the rear wheel

2 **Unhook the cable** and the cable-clamp bolt from the gear satellite, then let the satellite return to its resting position.

● You need both hands to do this – one to turn the gear satellite clockwise, and the other to remove the clamp bolt.

1 **Select first gear** and detach the cable and its outer from the cable-joint stopper, moving them outwards to unhook them.

● Unhook the cable and clamp bolt from the gear satellite as in Step 1 and 2 of Replacing a hub-gear cable.

4 **Insert the new cable** into the shifter and feed it through any lengths of cable outer to the hub gear.

● Thread the new cable through the cable-clamp bolt. Position the bolt the same distance from the cable outer as the measurement you took in Step 3, then tighten it.

● Reverse Step 2 to hook the cable-clamp bolt back in place.

2 **With a spanner on each** wheel nut, undo the wheel nuts on each side of the hub that hold the hub in the frame.

● Lift the rear wheel backwards and up, then lift the chain from the sprocket.

● Reverse Steps 1 and 2 to replace the wheel.

CHAIN, CASSETTE, AND CHAINSET

With every turn of the pedals the chain, cassette, and chainset are put under strain. The parts are in continual contact, and the motion of pedalling inevitably leads to wear. No matter how well you look after each part, they will eventually need removing and replacing.

How they work

The chain, cassette, and chainset combine to form the heart of the transmission, the part of the bike through which a rider's pedal power is transferred into forward motion. The pedals drive the chainset and, via the chain, turn a sprocket attached to the hub of the rear wheel, which in turn rotates the wheel.

Bikes with derailleur gears use mechs to shift the chain on to different-sized sprockets and chainrings, which make up the cassette and chainset. Each combination of chainring and sprocket provides a different gear ratio, giving up to 27 different gears that can be used to tackle anything from steep climbs to gentle flats.

Sprockets
Driven by the chain

Chain
Feeds through jockey wheels

Rear mech
Shifts the chain across the sprocket

EXPLODED CASSETTE

The cassette transfers the motion of the chain to the wheel. It consists of sprockets that slide on to the cassette body, which is bolted on to the hub. The cassette body houses the freewheel, which allows the wheel to turn when the cassette is stationary.

Cassette body
Contains the freewheel

Quick-release lever
Locks wheel into place

Lockring
Holds sprockets on the body

Sprocket
Slides on to cassette body

Profile
Secures sprockets to cassette body

Hub flange
Spokes connect hub to wheel rim

Spacer

CHAIN ANATOMY

The chain is the key to transmitting pedal power into forward motion.

To transfer power efficiently the chain must be strong, but flexible enough to fit securely around the teeth of the chainrings and sprockets. To achieve this, a series of links articulate around joining pins, which are surrounded by revolving metal barrels.

Joining pin
Connects inner and outer links

Barrel
Sits between teeth of chainrings and sprockets

Outer link
Shaped to allow quick gear shifts

Inner link
Rotates around the barrel

Rear wheel
Driven by the sprockets

Chainset
Powered by pedalling

Chainring
Carries the chain around the chainset

Pedal
Transmits energy to the chainset

Chain
Transmits power from the chainset

Lightweight components
The chain, cassette, and chainset are lightweight items that use the latest design and construction techniques to maximize strength and durability while maintaining an aerodynamic profile.

Chains

Replacing a chain is a regular maintenance task. All chains eventually wear out, even if you clean and lubricate them properly. A worn chain, as well as being inefficient, will quickly wear out other transmission parts, and so prove expensive. To determine how much a chain has worn, either use a specialist gauge from a bike shop or measure the length of 24 links. If the length is greater than 300mm (12in), the chain is worn.

New chains on derailleur gear systems are linked with a joining pin that comes with the chain. Or you can use a master link – effectively a two-part outer link that connects two inner links. The thicker chains of hub gears, BMX bikes, and some fixed-gear bikes are joined by split links (see p.75).

STEP LOCATOR

Parts of a Shimano chain and Master link

Shimano chain

Inner link

Master link

Outer link

Outer link

Pin

Pin

Outer link

Toolbox

- Chain-link extractor
- Long-nosed pliers

Replacing a derailleur chain

1 **Shift on to the smallest chainring** and sprocket so that the chain is slack.

- Place a link in the link extractor and push out the pin until the chain breaks.

- Remove the old chain with the link extractor.

3 **Remove the excess links** from the opposite end to the one on which there is a joining link. Leave an inner link so that the two ends can be joined together.

- Join the chain by pushing the pin of the joining link through the opposite inner link with the extractor tool.

Using a master link

2 **Thread a new chain** through the jockey wheels and around the biggest chainring and smallest sprocket.

● Pull the ends of the chain together so that there is a little tension in the jockey wheels. This establishes the length of chain you need.

1 **Follow Step 2** of Replacing a derailleur chain to thread the chain through the derailleurs and around the cogs and chainrings.

● Remove any excess links with a chain-link extractor, ensuring that both ends of the chain terminate with an inner link.

● Place the pin from each half of the master link into the inner links on each end of the chain.

4 **Loosen any stiff links** that occur when the chain links are compressed during Step 3.

● Flex the stiff links with a little sideways pressure until they become loose (*inset*).

● Remove the protruding part of the pin after joining a Shimano chain, as these have an extra-long joining pin.

● Break off the excess with long-nosed pliers.

2 **Pull the two ends** of the chain towards each other and loop each plate over the two pins (*inset*), then let go.

● The tension of the chain will draw the two halves of the master link back to the pins, seating them correctly and holding the chain together.

Fixie transmission

The beauty of the fixie bike is that it requires very little maintenance, apart from regular lubrication and safety checks. Some fixies have a "flip-flop" rear hub, which means that there is a single sprocket on either side of the rear hub. One is a fixed gear, which forms a "direct drive" between the pedals and sprocket. This means that if the pedals turn, so does the rear wheel, and vice versa. The other sprocket is a freewheel, meaning that the rider can stop pedalling and the rear wheel will still turn, "coasting" along using the bike's momentum.

You need to know how to remove a fixie's rear wheel in order to disengage a sprocket, re-engage the chain with the other sprocket, and refit the wheel. It's also useful to know how to fit fixie chains, which use a split link.

STEP LOCATOR

Parts of a split-link chain

Split-link pins

Groove

Split-link chain

Outer plate

Inner links

Split pin

Toolbox

- Spanners to fit wheel nuts
- Screwdriver (optional) • Long-nosed pliers

Swapping a flip-flop wheel

1 **Undo the rear wheel nuts** with a spanner on each one, turning both anti-clockwise.

- Once the wheel is loose in the drop-outs, push it forwards to create slack in the chain, then lift the chain off the sprocket (*inset*).

- Remove the wheel from the drop-outs by lifting it backwards.

3 **Pull the wheel backwards** in the drop-outs until there is just a little bit of slack in the chain.

- Finger-tighten the two wheel nuts (also known as "track nuts") that hold the wheel in place.

- Test the slack by lifting the chain with a screwdriver or spanner – there should be no more than 4mm (3/16in) of movement up and down.

Joining a split-link chain

Remove the chain from the chainset, then turn the wheel over to swap to the alternative gear – from the fixed gear to the freewheel, or vice versa.

- Hook the chain over the chosen sprocket, return the wheel to the bike, then replace the chain on the chainset.

Join the chain by pressing the side of the split link with the pins fixed in its plate through the two inner-link ends of the chain.

- Press the other plate on to the pins that are now sticking through the inner links.

Carefully tighten the wheel nuts, ensuring that the wheel stays centred in the bike frame.

- To do this, turn the spanners at the same time on each side, preserving the wheel's position in the drop-outs by avoiding any forward or backward pressure on the spanners.

- Repeat the screwdriver lift in Step 3 to check that the chain tension is still correct.

Push the split pin into the grooves of the split-link pins. These are sticking through the outer plate that you have just fitted. The split pin's open end should face the rear of the bike.

- Fix the split pin in place by pushing it home with long-nosed pliers until you feel it click.

Cassette and freewheel

The cassette and freewheel allow the rear wheel to rotate while the pedals remain stationary. Their internal mechanisms – the freehub body of a cassette and the block in a freewheel – will eventually wear out and need replacing. The sprockets on both can also wear. These parts will also need to be removed whenever you replace a broken spoke on the drive side of the rear wheel.

The tools for removing a freewheel and a cassette depend on the manufacturer of the part that is fitted to the bike. Usually, the manufacturer's name is stamped on the component. However, if you are in any doubt about which tool you need, take the wheel to the shop when buying a remover tool.

STEP LOCATOR

Parts of a freewheel and a cassette

Sprocket

Freewheel mechanism

Sprockets

Inner side ridges of cassette

Freewheel

Lockring

Cassette

Toolbox

- Spanners • Cassette remover • Chain whip
- Block remover • Grease

Removing a cassette

1 **Remove the quick-release skewer** from the rear wheel.

- Insert the cassette remover into the teeth of the lockring at the centre of the cassette.

- Replace the quick-release skewer to secure the cassette remover.

Removing a freewheel block

1 **Remove the quick-release skewer** and insert the block remover into the teeth at the block's centre.

- Lock the block remover in place by replacing the quick-release skewer.

Wrap the chain whip around a sprocket, and place the spanner on the remover.

● Press downwards on both tools. This holds the cassette, while the remover unlocks the lockring.

● Remove the quick-release skewer once the lockring starts turning.

● Continue to unscrew the lockring with the cassette remover.

Take off the smallest sprocket after you have removed the lockring. On many cassettes, the remaining sprockets come off in one piece. If they do not, you must put individual sprockets back in a certain way. Failure to do so will affect the precision of gear shifts. Usually, the sprockets are marked, so that lining up these marks ensures the correct sprocket orientation.

Put the spanner on the flats of the block remover and turn anticlockwise.

● As the block begins to move, remove the quick-release skewer and continue turning until the block comes off.

Check the integral freewheel mechanism, which is independent of the hub. Replace it with a new block if it is worn.

● Coat the threads of the hub with grease, then screw the block on by hand.

● Lock the block in place by tightening it with the spanner and the block remover.

Chainsets

Removing a chainset is a useful skill to have because it will allow you to replace an old crank, clean or replace a worn chainring, or work on the bottom bracket.

Chainsets are attached in one of four ways. Those on a hollow-axle bottom bracket can be removed with a specialist cap-bolt tool (*see Steps 1 and 2*). Chainsets with a self-removing Allen bolt can be detached with an 8mm Allen key (*see Step 3*). Versions with a standard Allen bolt can be detached with the relevant Allen key (*see Step 4*). Older chainsets with a hexagonal bolt can be removed with a chainset socket spanner.

When refitting a chainset, keep grease or oil from touching the axle. The chainset must be dry when fitted to the axle or it will work loose. After refitting, go for a short ride and then try the axle bolt again. If it is slightly loose, you should tighten it.

STEP LOCATOR

Parts of a chainset

Right-hand crank

Spider

Chainring bolt

Chainrings

Toolbox

- Cap-bolt tool and rubber mallet, Crank extractor, or 8mm Allen key ● 5mm Allen key
- Chainring-bolt peg-spanner

Removing a chainset

1 **For chainsets with a hollow-axle** bottom bracket, undo the left-hand crank cap bolt with a specialist cap-bolt tool.

- Insert the plastic head of the tool into the cap, using your fingers to grip the head's serrated edge. Turn the tool anti-clockwise.

- Take care as you remove the cap bolt, which is plastic and can easily be damaged.

4 **Use a long-handled Allen key** if there is an Allen bolt holding the chainset on your bike. Usually, an 8mm key is the size required.

- Work from below the chainset so that if you slip, the chainring teeth will not injure you.

- To remove the chainset, go to Step 5.

2 **Use an Allen key** to loosen the crank pinch bolt. After a few turns the crank can be pulled off the bottom-bracket axle – pull the crank towards you to leave the axle exposed.

● Hold the right-hand crank and give the exposed end of the bottom-bracket axle a sharp tap with a rubber mallet. The chainset will come away with the axle attached.

● To remove the chainrings, go to Step 6.

3 **Unscrew a self-removing Allen bolt** with an 8mm Allen key. These kinds of bolt extract the chainset as you unscrew them.

● Steady the crank with your free hand to give you something to push against. Work from below the chainset so that if your hand or the spanner slips, the chainring teeth will not injure you.

● To remove the chainrings, go to Step 6.

5 **Use a crank extractor** to remove the chainset if it is not the self-removing type. Make sure that the washer beneath the bolt has also been removed.

● Carefully screw the extractor into the delicate threads at the centre of the chainset. When the extractor is fully in, turn its handle clockwise to pull off the chainset.

● To remove the chainrings, go to Step 6.

6 **Remove the chainrings** with a 5mm Allen key on one side and a chainring-bolt peg-spanner to hold the bolt on the other. You can do this without taking the chainset off the axle, but you must remove it if you are working on the inner rings of some triple chainsets.

● Cure a creaking noise from the chainset by putting grease on the threads of the chainring bolts before you reassemble the chainset.

BOTTOM BRACKETS

There are three main types of bottom bracket: cartridge-bearing, hollow-axle, and press-fit. All use sealed bearings, which can wear out over time. If this happens on the cartridge version, replace the whole unit, but for the other types you only need to replace the bearings.

How they work

The bottom bracket joins the crank of each pedal with an axle, which rotates in the bike's frame. Each type of bracket consists of an axle, two bearings, and two cups (known as either the free cup and fixed cup, or the non-drive and drive-side cup). With the cartridge type, both cranks bolt onto the axle, but with the hollow-axle type, the drive-side crank is fixed to the axle and only the non-drive-side crank can be bolted on. The press-fit bottom bracket is just that – it is pressed inside the bottom-bracket shell with a specific tool to create a very tight fit. In engineering circles this is called an "interference" fit.

Providing strength
The axle and bearings of the bottom bracket need to be both strong and reliable enough to bear the weight and power of the rider.

CARTRIDGE-BEARING BOTTOM BRACKET ANATOMY

Each of the cartridge bearings is composed of ball-bearings, which are sandwiched in between an inner and outer race by plastic seals. The cartridge bearings are located close to each end of the bottom-bracket axle. A tubular sleeve fits over the two bearings, filling the space between them. The fixed and free cups fit over this sleeve to create a totally sealed unit.

Free cup
Screws into the bike's frame

Fixed cup
Holds the bottom bracket in place

Outer race
Houses the bearings

Ball-bearing
Supports the axle

Axle
Connects the cranks and rotates in the bearings

Crank
Turns the axle

HOLLOW-AXLE BOTTOM BRACKET ANATOMY

The drive-side crank is permanently fixed to the axle, which passes through both cups. The non-drive side crank slides onto the axle and is secured by two pinch bolts. The crank cap bolt inserts into the end of the axle to hold the crank against a cartridge bearing, ensuring there is no play, rather like the stem cap bolt on a threadless headset (see p.100).

Pinch bolts
Hold crank in place on the axle

Crank cap bolt
Presses crank against bearings

Cartridge bearing
Lets the axle turn

Cup
Holds bearings in the frame

Crank
Turns the axle

Cup
Holds the bearings in place in the frame

Axle
Connects the cranks together and rotates in the bearings

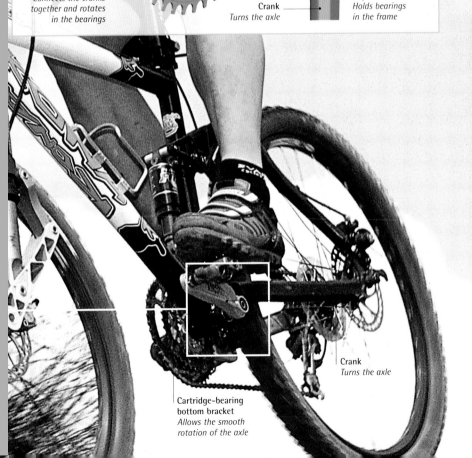

Crank
Turns the axle

Cartridge-bearing bottom bracket
Allows the smooth rotation of the axle

Cartridge bottom bracket

Cartridge bottom brackets require no routine maintenance. Their bearings are sealed from the elements – even from the water you use for hosing or pressure-washing your bike, provided that you turn the pedals forwards during the wash.

When the bearings do eventually wear out you will have to replace the whole unit. The remover tools for this job are specific to each particular bottom bracket, so check which make is fitted to your bike before buying the tools.

If you are planning a replacement, there are three types of bottom bracket axle to choose: square-tapered, Shimano Octalink, and Isis. The type used in the steps in this sequence is square-tapered; the type shown below is Octalink.

Finally, if you are having any problems installing a bottom bracket on your bike, ask the experts at a bike shop to help you.

STEP LOCATOR

Parts of a cartridge bottom bracket

Drive (fixed-cup) side

Non-drive (free-cup) side

Bottom-bracket axle

Toolbox

• Measuring callipers • Ruler • Spanner
• Cartridge bottom bracket remover • Grease

Installing a cartridge bottom bracket

1 **Put the bike on a workstand** and remove the chainset (see pp.78–9).

• Use a pair of callipers to measure the length of the old axle before you remove the bottom bracket, so that you can be sure the replacement has an axle of the same length. You need to do this because different chainsets are designed to work with different axle lengths.

4 **Grease the threads** of each side of the new bottom bracket for easier fitting. The non-drive threads are sometimes referred to as the free-cup and the drive-side threads are known as the fixed cup. Do not grease the drive side of a bottom bracket with Italian threads.

2 **Measure the width of the bottom-bracket** shell with a ruler. The shell forms part of the bike's frame and will be either 68mm (2¾in) or 73mm (3in) wide. This width determines the width of the bracket unit you need to buy.

3 **Remove both the cranks** (see pp.78–9), insert a bottom-bracket remover into the non-drive side of the bracket and turn the remover anticlockwise with a spanner.

● Repeat on the other side, turning clockwise. Turn it anticlockwise if your bike has an Italian-threaded bottom bracket (marked 36 x 1).

5 **Insert the bottom bracket** from the drive (fixed-cup) side using the remover tool. Fit the teeth of the tool into the indentations of the bottom bracket (see enlargement).

● Insert the non-drive (free-cup) side when the drive side is almost in position. Use the remover to screw it in a few turns. Fully tighten the drive side, then the non-drive side.

Hollow-axle bottom bracket

Hollow-axle bottom brackets, such as those made by SRAM, Campagnolo, and Shimano, are designed to increase bottom-bracket strength. The axle bearings screw onto the outside of the bottom-bracket shell, which houses a large-diameter axle that is hollow, light, and stronger than other axles. Since the bearings are further apart than on other bottom-bracket designs, they encounter less torque, which increases their lifespan. But they will eventually wear out, so you will need to know how to remove and replace them. The steps can also be followed if you want to upgrade to this system.

STEP LOCATOR

Parts of a hollow-axle bottom bracket

Chainring

Axle

Combined drive-side cup and sleeve

Left-hand crank

Spacers

Non-drive side cup

Pinch bolt

Crank cap bolt

Toolbox

● Hollow-axle cup tool ● Hollow-axle crank cap tool ● Allen key multi-tool

Installing a hollow-axle bottom bracket

1 **The faces of the** bottom bracket shell must be flat and parallel. This requires specialist equipment, so get the frame checked at a bike shop.

● Measure the width of the bottom bracket shell, then check the manufacturer's instructions to determine how many spacers are required and on which cup to put them.

● Grease the threads of the cups and place the necessary spacers on them.

4 **Push the left-hand** crank onto the end of the axle, matching the wide notch on the axle with the wide tooth on the crank. This ensures the cranks are mounted at 180 degrees.

● Unlike other bottom brackets, a dry interface between crank and axle is not necessary. Put a little grease on the axle before you fit the crank.

● Campagnolo's hollow-axle bottom bracket fits in a similar way, but has a split axle (*inset*).

2 **Screw the cups into** the frame as far as you can with your fingers (*inset*).

● The drive-side cup screws in anticlockwise, and the non-drive side cup screws in clockwise.

● Secure the cups on each side by tightening them with the hollow-axle cup tool (*main image*).

● Grease the axle in preparation for pushing it through the cups.

3 **Hold the drive side** (right-hand) crank and push the axle through the hole in the centre of the drive-side cup.

● Continue pushing until the end of the axle pops out of the non-drive side cup.

● You may encounter resistance, especially as you push the axle through the non-drive side cup. If this happens, give the centre of the crank a sharp tap with a plastic mallet.

5 **Grease the threads** of the crank cap bolt, and screw it into place with your fingers.

● Tighten the crank cap bolt with the crank cap tool, which draws the crank onto the axle.

● Do not over-tighten the crank cap bolt. Rotate the cranks and if the axle is stiff, loosen the crank cap bolt a little.

6 **Tighten the crank** pinch bolts with an Allen key to fix the crank in place.

● The pinch bolts work as a pair, so must be equally tight. Tighten them in sequence by screwing in the first a little, then screwing in the other by the same amount. Repeat until both bolts are tight, but do not use excessive force.

● If you have access to a torque wrench, use it to tighten the bolts to the manufacturer's instructions.

Press-fit bottom bracket

A relatively new innovation, this type of bottom bracket is lighter, simpler, and cheaper than other designs. "Press-fit" refers to the way the bearing cups and bearings fit inside the bottom-bracket shell. The cups don't screw in using shell threads, as most brackets do, but achieve an "interference" fit – an engineering term for a very tight fit – by being pressed in. The bearings are then pressed into the cups, and the axle and cranks bolt through the bearings.

Press-fit bottom brackets require little maintenance, since they are usually protected by good seals. Replacing the bearings is relatively easy, but requires a bearing-puller tool to remove the old set and a bearing press, or similar device, to fit the new ones.

STEP LOCATOR

Parts of a press-fit bottom bracket

- Chainring
- Drive-side crank
- Drive-side axle
- Non-drive-side bearing
- Drive-side bearing
- Non-drive-side crank
- Retaining rings
- Non-drive-side axle

Toolbox

- Allen key multi-tool • Bearing puller • Bearing press • Rubber mallet • Circlip- or snap-ring pliers, or small screwdriver

Servicing a press-fit bottom bracket

1 **Remove the chainset** using an Allen key (*inset*) or the correct tool for the crank on your bike (*see pp.78-9*).

- Remove the drive- and non-drive-side cranks from the bottom bracket.

- If the cranks have a one-piece axle, it might require a sharp knock with a rubber mallet to dislodge it from the bearings.

4 **Remove the old bearing,** which should be in place inside the bearing-puller tool.

- Repeat Steps 2 and 3 to remove the non-drive-side bearing.

- Inspect the retaining rings for damage (*inset*), and if necessary, remove and replace them using circlip- or snap-ring pliers, or a small screwdriver.

- Clean the bearing cups with degreaser solution.

2 **Insert the bearing puller** behind the drive-side bearing (*inset*), ensuring it doesn't snag on the retaining ring, which prevents the bearings being inserted too far during fitting.

- There are several types of bearing-puller tools, each of which work slightly differently. In this case, a sleeve covers the bottom-bracket shell while a nut holds the bearing puller against the bearing.

- Assemble the rest of the bearing-puller tool.

3 **Thread the nut** onto the bearing puller by hand, then tighten it with an adjustable spanner to secure the bearing puller flush against the bearing.

- Using an Allen key, turn the bearing puller to extract the bearing from the drive side of the bottom bracket, while holding the nut in place with an adjustable spanner.

5 **With your fingers**, press the new drive-side bearing into the drive-side cup inside the bottom-bracket shell, ensuring that you insert it straight and level into the cup.

- Insert the bearing press from the drive side.

- Press a new bearing into the non-drive-side cup, exactly as you did on the drive side.

6 **Place the non-drive-side** of the bearing press onto the central thread, tightening it up to the non-drive-side bearing with your fingers.

- Turn the bearing-press handle on the drive side until the bearings go all the way into the bottom bracket, and are flush with the face of the shell.

- Add any dust seals particular to the bottom bracket, then reverse Step 1 to refit the chainset.

PEDALS

There are two types of pedal, flat and clipless. Pedals with open bearings require regular inspection and lubrication. Clipless pedals must be lubricated to ensure easy foot release. Cleats should be correctly fitted to the rider's shoes and regularly inspected for wear.

How they work

The two pedals transfer the push from the rider's legs and feet into both cranks which, in turn, rotate the axle in the bottom bracket. The body of a pedal rotates around an axle and is supported on bearings that are either open or held within a cartridge. The pedal's axle screws into the crank.

Pedals should grip a rider's feet in some way. For example, studs that prevent foot slippage will help a rider who makes frequent stops, such as a commuter in heavy traffic. Some flat pedals are fitted with toe-clips and straps that hold the front of the foot, although they can interfere with the foot as the rider tries to remove it. Clipless pedals hold the foot securely, while releasing it easily whenever the rider wants.

Converting energy
Pedals are the invention that defines cycling. They are the first step in the process of converting human energy into mechanical motion.

FLAT PEDAL ANATOMY

Two bearings on the pedal's axle are held in place by a cone and lockring that screw on to the outer end of the axle. A knurled retainer attaches the pedal body to the axle. The cone (not visible) and the lockring can be adjusted to permit the free rotation of the body around the axle, without any play.

Crank
Transfers power to the bottom bracket

Pedal body
Rotates on the axle

Locknut
Holds the cone in place

Axle
Screws into the crank

Knurled retainer
Holds the body on to the axle

Ball-bearings
Allow the body to rotate around the axle

Pedal
*Connects the rider's foot
to the transmission*

Pedal axle

The axle of a pedal is usually made from steel and the cranks from aluminium alloy. This creates an interface between the two metals where a chemical reaction can take place, so it is important that you coat the threads with grease before you put pedals on your bike. The tools to remove the axles are specific to the make of the pedals, and will be either supplied with the pedals or available at a good bike shop.

Most pedals contain two bearings on which the pedal body revolves around its axle. These sometimes need replacing; in the case of ball-bearings, they need regular cleaning, checking, and greasing.

Pedal axles can be damaged by an impact or during a fall, and a bent axle can cause riding discomfort or even injury. After removing the pedals, rotate their axles by hand, feeling for the tight spots that are evidence of a bent axle.

STEP LOCATOR

1 2 3 4 5 6

Parts of a pedal

Cleat-release mechanism

Pedal body

Pedal axle

Retainer

Spanner flats

Release tension adjuster

Toolbox
- 15mm bike spanner ● Allen key multi-tool
- Remover tool ● Degreaser ● Grease

Removing and lubricating a pedal axle

1 **Place a spanner** on the flats of the axle to remove a pedal.

● Turn the spanner anticlockwise for the right pedal, which has a right-hand thread, and clockwise for the left pedal, which has a left-hand thread.

● Steady the opposite crank with your hand to give you something to push against.

4 **Lift the axle from the pedal** once you have fully unscrewed the retainer nut.

● Clean the axle with degreaser and inspect it. If the axle is bent, it will need replacing.

● Replace the bearings on the end of the axle if they are worn.

Hold the removed pedal, with the axle upwards, in a vice.

● Remove the axle by using a remover tool that fits over the knurled retainer connecting the axle to the pedal.

Ensure that the remover tool fits snugly on to the retainer. The retainer may be damaged if you do not.

● Place a spanner on the flats of the remover tool in place and turn it to remove the retainer.

● Turn the spanner clockwise for the right axle retainer, which has a left-hand thread, and anticlockwise for the left axle retainer, which has a right-hand thread.

Hold the cone with one spanner and remove the locknut with another. The cone and locknut hold the bearings on the end of the axle.

● Remove the cone, then the old bearings. Clean the end of the axle.

● Set the new bearings in grease and screw the cone back on top of them. Then lock the cone with the locknut.

Grease the inner bearing to prolong its life. If it is worn, the whole axle assembly must be replaced.

● Push some grease down into the bearing after cleaning the axle. To reassemble the pedal, repeat Steps 1–4 in reverse order.

Clipless pedals

Clipless pedals were developed in response to the racing cyclist's need to apply power throughout the entire pedal revolution. They hold the foot to the pedal by locking on to a cleat attached to the sole of the shoe. The mechanism that holds the cleat is spring-loaded – the foot is released by turning the heel outwards.

The release spring is an essential working part and must be kept clean and well lubricated. Use light oils on road pedals and heavier oils on off-road pedals. Wipe oil from the pedal body to stop your foot from slipping. The mechanism lets the foot pivot around its long axis during each revolution. The oil applied to the release spring is enough to keep the mechanism working well.

Toolbox
- 15mm bike spanner ● Allen key multi-tool
- Degreaser ● Stiff brush ● Oil

ROAD PEDALS

Road pedals are light, supportive, and, because of the greater speeds involved in road riding, aerodynamic. They need to engage and release the feet with equal ease as well as holding the foot securely. Ideally, you should be able to adjust them according to how much movement your feet make during pedalling.

Time road pedal
These pedals offer a range of movement that can be adjusted to suit the requirements of individual riders. Keep them well maintained by scrubbing regularly with degreaser, using a stiff brush. Wash this off, then lubricate the release spring with heavier oil, dribbling it from a can.

Top face

Bottom face

Pedal body

Retention mechanism

Release spring

Release-tension adjuster

Look road pedal
These easy-to-maintain pedals have a small Allen bolt on top of the back plate retention mechanism, which adjusts the foot-release tension. The pedals need to be scrubbed clean regularly. Occasionally, dribble some oil between the back plate and pedal body.

Top face

Pedal body

Bottom face

Release-tension adjuster

Release spring

Back plate

OFF-ROAD PEDALS

Off-road pedals are fitted with retention mechanisms on at least two sides so that the rider's feet can attach to the pedal no matter which way up it is. The pedals also let mud pass through to prevent them from becoming clogged.

Time off-road pedal

The few moving parts of this simple pedal are protected in the body of the pedal. Keep the parts clean and dribble a little heavy oil into the point where the release bar enters the pedal body. If necessary, replace the bearings and axles (*see pp.90–1*).

Retention spring

Top face

Bottom face

Release-tension adjuster

Retention bar

Axle thread

Shimano off-road pedal

The open design of this pedal allows good mud clearance but exposes the pedal's retention mechanism to the elements. Clean and degrease the pedals regularly and lubricate the moving parts with a heavy lubricant. The release-tension adjuster is on the back plate of this double-sided pedal.

Top face

Release-tension adjuster

Bottom face

Release spring

Retention mechanism

Crank Brothers pedal

This is an open design with excellent mud clearance and very few moving parts – the retention mechanism is just a simple spring. Clean the pedals regularly, and very occasionally re-grease the bearings using a grease gun and a special adaptor that is sold with the pedals.

Retention spring

Plan view

Axle thread

Retention bar

Retention bar

Profile view

Pedal axle

Retention spring

Pedal cleats

Clipless pedals are designed to hold your feet firmly in place, so it is important that the cleats on the pedals are positioned correctly on the sole of your shoes. The right position also enables you to transfer the maximum amount of leg power into the pedals.

Once you have set up the cleats, you might find that your feet try to return to their natural position as you ride. Alter the cleat's angle to accommodate this. However, do not alter its fore and aft position because the position shown here is the most efficient for applying power to the pedals.

The steps in this sequence show an off-road pedal (*see pp.92–3*), but the principles are the same for road pedals.

STEP LOCATOR

Parts of a pedal cleat

In-shoe threads for fixing bolts

Cleat

Fixing bolts

Recessed cleat plate

Toolbox

- White marker pen • Silicone sealant
- Allen keys • Screwdriver

Fitting a pedal cleat

1 **Put on your cycling shoes** and mark them on the outer side where your foot is widest. This point is usually slightly behind the smallest toe and is in line with the ball of the foot. The aim of setting up a cleat is to make sure that this part of your foot is exactly above the pedal axle when you ride.

4 **Put on your cycling shoes** and sit on your bike, engaging the cleats in the pedals.

- Ask someone to check from the side that the initial mark you made is over the pedal axle.

- Go for a ride and check whether your feet try to turn in or out on the pedals.

Take off your shoes and continue the mark you made with a straight line across the sole of your shoe, from outside to inside. This line must be at right angles to the initial mark and should end on the inner side of the shoe, in line with the initial mark.

Place the cleat on the shoe so that the line runs exactly through its centre. Some cleats are marked to help with this alignment.

● Make sure that the horizontal axis of the cleat is exactly parallel with the line you made.

● Secure the cleat in place with the screws or Allen bolts provided.

Adjust the cleats to accommodate any foot position changes your test ride reveals, but keep the cleat centre over the axle.

● Mark the sole of your shoes all around the cleat, so that you can line it up again.

● Remove the cleat, put anti-seize compound on the screw threads and line the cleat up with the marks you made. Tighten the cleat.

Seal the Allen heads on the bolts that secure the cleats to off-road shoes. These heads can fill with grit, causing them to lose shape and making it difficult to replace the cleats when they wear down. Prevent this by filling the Allen heads with blobs of a silicone sealant available from DIY shops.

STEERING AND WHEELS

Steering gives you control of a bike's handling and direction. Regularly check and maintain the headset, handlebar, wheels, and hubs to safeguard their reliability at all times.

HEADSETS

A headset allows the bike to be steered. The headset must be properly adjusted to allow smooth, safe steering and to prolong its life. The bearings and bearing surfaces need regular inspection and lubrication and anything that is worn must be replaced at once.

How they work

The main function of the headset is to enable the rider to change the direction of the front wheel under any conditions. There are two types of headset, threaded and threadless, and both hold the front fork securely in the head tube, while simultaneously allowing the fork to turn freely.

The headset rotates on bearings, which are held in place by cups, one above the head tube, the other below. For the forks to turn freely, these two cups press on the bearings just enough to prevent any play in the part of the fork known as the steerer tube. The way this pressure (also known as load) is achieved varies between the threaded and threadless headsets.

THREADLESS HEADSET ANATOMY

The stem cap bolt at the top of a threadless headset screws into a star washer below. Some types of threadless headset contain a wedge instead of a star washer. When the stem cap bolt is turned with an Allen key, it pushes the stem and spacer down on to the bearings in both the top and bottom cups, and pulls up the steerer tube at the same time. This places sufficient load on the bearings for the fork to turn freely with no play. The stem is secured in place on the steerer by tightening two clamp bolts (not visible on the illustration).

Stem clamp bolts
Clamp stem to steerer tube

Star washer
Grips the steerer tube

Stem cap bolt
Pulls the steerer tube upwards

Stem
Links handlebar and headset

Spacer
Sits on top of the bearings

Top cup
Loads the bearings

Top bearings
Allow the steerer tube to turn in the headset

Bottom cup
Loads the bearings

Steerer tube
Connects the fork to the headset

Bottom bearings
Allow the fork to turn

Fork crown
Turns the fork

THREADED HEADSET ANATOMY

Screwing the top cup down the thread of the steerer places a load on the top bearings to the point where the forks turn freely but without play. The cup, and consequently the front fork, is then locked in place by a lockring that also screws down the threaded steerer. The stem is attached to the headset by tightening the stem's expander bolt, which pulls up a wedge and jams the stem's quill inside the threaded steerer.

Stem
Links the handlebar and headset

Quill
Fits inside the threaded steerer

Expander bolt
Draws up the wedge

Lockring
Locks the top cup in place

Top bearings
Allow the steerer to turn in the headset

Top cup
Loads the bearings

Threaded steerer
Connects the headset to the fork

Wedge
Jams the quill in the steerer

Bottom bearings
Allow the fork to turn

Handlebar
Steers the front wheel

Headset
Holds the fork in the head tube

Fork
Holds and turns the front wheel

Steering effectively

A headset allows the rider to steer the front wheel effectively and confidently. The handlebar, which is connected to the steerer tube by the stem, turns the fork and the front wheel.

Threadless headset

To determine whether your bike is equipped with a threadless or a threaded headset, look at the stem. If you can see bolts on the side of the part that sits on top of the head tube, it is a threadless headset.

A number of different types of threadless headset can be fitted to modern bikes. These range from the type that has both top and bottom cups, like the traditional headset, to others, such as the headset illustrated here, where the bearing surfaces fit inside the head tube. All the various types of headset work on the same principle and are taken apart in a similar way.

Occasionally, you need to strip down the headset in order to check it for wear and to clean and lubricate the bearings. If you find any cups or bearing surfaces are worn, you will need to replace the whole headset. This job requires specialist equipment and is best left to the experts in a good bike shop.

Adjusting and cleaning a threadless headset

1 **Remove the stem cap bolt** from the centre of the stem cap with an Allen key. This bolt loads the headset to prevent play in it, rather than securing the stem.

STEP LOCATOR

Parts of a threadless headset

Stem cap
Top bearing cover
Stem cap bolt
Top race
Bottom cup

Toolbox
● Allen key multi-tool ● Degreaser ● Grease

4 **Lower the fork** and lift off the top spacers and either the top cup or bearing cover, depending on the type of threadless headset.

● Clean, degrease, and look at the bottom bearing. If there are no signs of wear, grease the bearing.

● Take the centring wedge out of the head tube. Clean the bearings, bearing surfaces (inset), and bearing cover or top cup . Examine for wear, put new grease on the bearings and re-install.

2 **Loosen the clamp bolts** on the side of the stem once you have removed the cap bolt. The stem and handlebar assembly are now free. It is the stem clamp bolts that secure the stem to the steerer.

3 **Take hold of the front fork,** then lift the stem and handlebar from the steerer. You can leave these to hang out of the way, supported by the brake and gear cables.

5 **Put the fork back** into the head tube and replace the centring wedge, bearing cover, and spacers.

● Put the handlebar and stem back on top of the steerer.

● Load the headset by tightening the stem cap bolt to a point where the handlebar turns freely, but there is no play in the headset. Secure the stem in place by tightening the clamp bolts.

● Apply the front brake and try to push the bike forwards to check that the headset is not loose.

Threaded headset

Older bikes and children's bikes are equipped with threaded headsets. This type of headset is designed to make it easy to raise and lower the stem whenever you want to change the height of the handlebar and adjust your riding position.

The headset's top cup and the locknut that holds it in place are both screwed on to the steerer. The stem is equipped with a shaft, or quill, that fits inside the steerer. For safety reasons, you should never raise a stem above the limit marked on its quill.

On some even older headsets the top cup screws down. Its serrated top edge is held in place by a clamp bolt on a similarly serrated lockring assembly. When the clamp bolt is loosened, the top cup screws off.

Remember to disconnect the brakes before you start working on the headset and make sure that you reconnect them when you have finished. Before the stem is replaced into the steerer of the headset, coat the quill with grease (see pp.38–9).

STEP LOCATOR

Parts of a threaded headset

Spacer
Top race
Locknut
Top cup
SHIMANO ULTEGRA
Bottom cup
Fork crown race
SHIMANO ULTEGRA

Toolbox

● 6mm Allen key ● Grease ● Degreaser ● 30mm and 32mm headset spanners ● Plastic mallet

Servicing a threaded headset

1 **Undo the Allen bolt** in the stem centre and knock it downwards with a plastic mallet to free the steerer. The stem is secured into the steerer by an expander bolt which, as it is tightened, draws a wedge up inside the quill.

● Lift the stem from the steerer.

4 **Degrease all the bearing surfaces** of the top and bottom cups, and of the races. You can access the top bearings by pushing the fork up the head tube and holding it there.

● Inspect the bearing surfaces and if any are damaged, you need to fit a new headset – this is best left to a good bike shop.

2 **Unscrew the locknut** while holding the top cup still with a headset spanner.

- Spread newspaper on the floor to catch loose bearings that may drop out of the top cup.
- Lift off the spacers, then unscrew the top cup upwards from the steerer.

3 **Lower the fork** to reveal the bearings in the bottom cup. Screwing the top cup upwards allows this to happen. Although most headsets have ball-bearings held in cages, watch out for loose bearings that may drop out of the bottom cup. Some headsets have roller bearings – treat these as ball-bearings in the following steps.

5 **Grease both the top and bottom bearings** or set loose bearings in grease inside each cup.

- Completely unscrew the top cup to remove the bearings. Set the bearings individually in the greased cups and screw the top cup back on. Bearings held in cages can be greased in situ so long as they are not worn out.

6 **Screw the top cup down** on to the top bearings. Replace the spacers and locknut.

- Adjust the top cup so that steering is free.
- Pull the fork to check there is no forward movement in the headset.
- Replace the spacer, hold the top cup with a spanner, and tighten the locknut on to it.
- Replace the stem and handlebar.

HANDLEBARS

Most modern bikes are fitted with either straight or drop handlebars. A rider must be able to rely totally on the handlebar, so for safety reasons, a handlebar must be replaced at once if scratches, stress marks, or cracks develop on the surface.

Straight handlebar

Owners of road bikes sometimes want to change the handlebar to a different shape, often to suit the proportions of their body or because of their cycling needs. Some cyclists want to replace a drop handlebar with a straight, or flat, bar. Others may want to replace their existing straight bars with riser bars, or vice versa. Riser bars, which are fitted to mountain bikes, are straight in the centre, then rise up to become straight where the grips are. They are fitted the same way as a straight handlebar.

The steps in this sequence apply to all straight handlebars, whatever the reason for replacing them. However, when replacing a drop handlebar with a straight bar, it will necessary to swap the brake levers for levers that work with flat or riser bars. Some of these steps will also be useful when fitting new grips, brake levers, gear-shifters, or bar-ends to an existing handlebar.

Parts of a straight handlebar

Plastic plug

Grip

Straight handlebar

Ring clamp

Bar-end

Shifter unit

Brake lever

Clamp bolt

Toolbox

- Half-round file ● Emery paper ● Ruler
- Allen key multi-tool ● Hairspray

STEP LOCATOR

1 2 3 4 5

Fitting a straight handlebar

1 **Remove any raised bit of metal** inside the stem clamp with a medium, half-round file (inset). Smooth the area with emery paper.

- Place the straight handlebar into the stem clamp and screw in the clamp bolts. Check that the bar is centred before tightening it fully. If you are fitting a riser bar, decide what angle of sweep you want it to be before tightening the bolts.

2 **Secure the ring clamp** of the brake lever to the handlebar. Like road brake levers, off-road levers have a ring clamp that fits over and secures them to the handlebar. Some off-road brake levers have integrated shift levers with only one clamp. However, some are separate so there are two clamps to go over the handlebar.

3 **Spray hairspray** into the handlebar grips to help the grips to slide on to the handlebar. When the hairspray dries, the grips will fit tightly to the handlebars.

4 **Slide the grips** on to the handlebar while they are still wet with hairspray.

● Push the grips further on if you are fitting bar-ends to allow for the width of the bar-end clamp.

● Fit grip-locks to hold the grips in place and prevent them from twisting while you are riding.

5 **Clamp on the bar-ends.** Line them up parallel with the angle of your stem to begin with, then adjust their angle to suit your own preference after riding.

● Put a plastic plug in each end of the handlebar to prevent injury in the event of a fall.

Drop handlebar

Road riding cyclists often fit drop handlebars to their bikes so their bodies can adopt a lower, more aerodynamic posture. However, the handlebar should never be positioned so low that breathing is restricted when holding the bottom of the handlebars.

Replace a drop handlebar at once if any cracks develop on its surface. The steps in this sequence will show how to replace a drop handlebar and how to fit, and therefore how to re-position, brake levers. Cyclists with larger hands and long arms may prefer to mount the levers lower down the handlebar than the ideal position shown here.

Regularly replace the handlebar tape as shown in Steps 5 and 6, and insert a plug in each end of the handlebar after taping to prevent possible injury in a fall.

Brake levers for flat handlebars will not work on drop handlebars, and may not work with all brake types. Check the compatibility of your components before swapping.

STEP LOCATOR

Parts of a drop handlebar

Drop handlebar   Cable groove

Handlebar tape

Brake lever hood   Rubber cover   Brake lever

Toolbox

- Half-round file ● Emery paper
- Allen key multi-tool

Fitting a drop handlebar

1 **Use a medium, half-round file** to remove any raised areas of metal inside the part of the stem that clamps the bar in place. These raised areas can bite into the handlebar, eventually causing them to fracture.

- Smooth the filed surface with emery paper.

4 **Secure the levers** of a Campagnolo brake/shift to the handlebar by tightening a bolt on the outside of the hood with an Allen key. Pull the lever hood cover forwards to access the bolt. The bolt on Shimano levers is further down the outer side of the lever hood so that you need to put your Allen key into a recess under the rubber cover.

Fit the new handlebar and tighten up the clamp bolts. Before you secure the bolts, try to line up the flat part of the bottom of the handlebar with a point just below the back brake.

Slide the steel ring of the brake lever over the handlebar. This ring clamps the lever to the handlebar.

● Attach the bolt in the brake lever hood to the screw thread on the ring and tighten.

Pull the cover of the brake lever hood forwards and place a short length of tape over each steel ring.

● Wind the tape in one turn from the bottom to the top of the lever hood. When you reach the top of the handlebar, secure the tape with insulating tape.

Start taping at one end of the handlebar.

● Wind upwards, covering half of the previous turn with each subsequent turn.

● Keep the tape tight at all times.

Tri-bars

If you want to compete in a time trial or a triathlon, or want to achieve a more aerodynamic riding position, you could fit tri-bars to the existing handlebar on your bike. Tri-bars do not provide the same aerodynamic advantage of the integrated tri-bars used on triathlon- or time-trial-specific bikes, but they do provide a high percentage of it.

Tri-bars are simple to fit, and they can be removed easily by undoing the fixing-clamp bolts shown in Step 1. Once fitted, tri-bars must be checked regularly to ensure that the bolts remain tight. Also, test all bolts for tightness with an Allen key after your first ride on them. However, be careful not to over-tighten them – sufficient force to stop the bolts moving is all that is required.

STEP LOCATOR

Parts of a tri-bar

Tri-bar extension

Fixing clamp

Arm rest

Pad

Toolbox

• Allen key multi-tool • Insulation tape (optional)

Installing a tri-bar

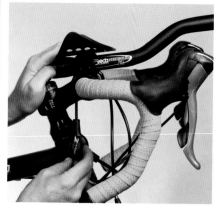

1 **Assemble the tri-bars** from their component parts.

• Position the tri-bars on the middle of the handlebar, ensuring each one is placed the same distance from either side of the stem.

• Tighten the clamp bolt on each tri-bar with an Allen key, but don't fit the pads yet.

• You can wrap insulation tape around your handlebar before fitting the tri-bars, to prevent it from being scratched by the clamps.

4 **Attach the pads** to the arm rests. These are usually affixed using sticky-backed velcro.

• Peel off the backing and stick the velcro to the metal arm rest, then fit the pad. You can remove and reposition the pad until you find a comfortable position.

2 **Set the arm rests** in the furthest apart position, using an Allen key on the bolts that secure them in position.

● The arm rests will either fit on the tri-bar extensions, or onto the handlebar itself to the outside of the tri-bar extensions.

3 **Your arms should be** fairly wide apart when you sit in an aerodynamic tuck position, so that they don't restrict your breathing.

● Get somebody to help you or use a mirror. Your hands should be close together, but your upper arms should be as close to vertical as possible.

● Move the arm rests to achieve the pictured body position by moving the rests in or out, then reattaching them (*inset*).

5 **Adjust the reach** of the tri-bar extensions until you achieve a riding position where your elbow joint is flexed at an angle of 90 degrees.

● Most tri-bar extensions can be moved forwards and backwards by undoing an Allen-key clamp bolt.

HUBS

There are two types of hub, open-bearing and cartridge. The cones and bearings of open-bearing hubs must be adjusted to let the hubs spin freely, with little play. The bearings in both types of hub need regular checking and lubricating.

How they work

The hub allows the wheel to revolve. Quick-release mechanisms or nuts secure the axle into the bike's frame. The axle remains static while the hub body spins around on bearings. Spokes run from the hub's flanges to the rim of the wheel – as the hub spins, so does the rim.

The transmission transfers the rider's power from the pedals to the rear wheel, while the front wheel is essentially pushed along by the revolutions of the rear. The gears on a bike are located on the rear hub, either as a hub-gear unit or as multiple sprockets in the case of derailleur gears.

The freewheel mechanism, which is also on the rear hub, allows a rider to cease pedalling while the bike is in motion – for example, on a downhill stretch of road. This mechanism is part of the hub in both hub gears and hubs with cassette sprockets.

Minimizing friction
Free-spinning hubs are an essential part of an efficient bike. Their bearings must create as little friction as possible, so as not to slow the rider's forward progress.

EXPLODED CARTRIDGE HUB

The axle of a cartridge hub is not threaded, so the bearings are pushed on to each end of the axle and covered by a seal. When the hub is assembled, the bearings sit in the hub body, just to the outside of the flanges, with the axle running through them. Lockrings ensure that everything is held in place.

Axle
Rotates the wheel

Flange
Anchors the spokes to the hub

Seal
Covers the bearings

Hub body
Contains the axle

Cartridge bearings
Support the hub body

**Open-bearing
front hub**
*Allows the wheel to
revolve smoothly*

OPEN-BEARING FRONT HUB ANATOMY

The body on an open-bearing front hub spins on ball-bearings
that are set within, and at each end of, the hub body. Each set
of bearings is held in place by a cone (not visible) that is screwed
down on the thread at the end of the axle. A locknut (not visible)
locks the cone in place on the same thread. If the hub is held by a
quick-release mechanism, the axle is hollow to allow the quick-
release skewer to go through it.

Axle
*Remains static
as the wheel
revolves*

Hub body
*Rotates
around
the axle*

**Ball-
bearings**
*Support the
hub body*

**Quick-release
skewer**
*Locks the axle
in place*

Open-bearing hub

Hubs are available in two types – open-bearing or cartridge. The open-bearing hubs require much more maintenance than the cartridge type, since their bearings need regular inspection, cleaning, and regreasing. As a result, the ability to strip down and service an open-bearing hub is a skill that can be used repeatedly.

The following steps will help you to remove an axle and a freehub, as well as regrease and retighten the bearings. They can be applied to a Shimano front or rear hub and a Campagnolo front hub. However, leave servicing a Campagnolo rear hub to the experts at a bike shop because it requires specialist tools.

If you are working on a rear hub, you need to remove the cassette by following the steps on pp.76–7 before tackling the steps in this sequence.

STEP LOCATOR

Parts of an open-bearing hub

Locknut   Flange   Flange   Freehub body
        Cone   Hub   Locknut
                  body

Spacers   Axle

Non-drive side   Drive side

Toolbox

- 15mm and 16mm cone spanners (Shimano)
- 13mm and 14mm cone spanners (Campagnolo)
- Grease • Grease gun (optional)
- Allen key multi-tool • Adjustable spanner
- 8mm or 10mm Allen key

Overhauling an open-bearing hub

1 **Remove** the locknut on the drive side with a spanner while holding the non-drive side cone with a cone spanner. Some locknuts can be removed with an ordinary spanner, others with an Allen key.

- Keep holding the non-drive side cone with the cone spanner and remove the drive-side cone with another cone spanner.

4 **Fit a new hub body** or the cleaned old one by reversing Step 3.

- Re-insert the axle from the non-drive side. Tighten the drive cone up to the bearings and check that the axle spins freely with minimal play.

- Lock the cone into position with the locknut. Use the cone spanners to check that the non-drive cone is tight against its locknut.

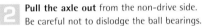

Pull the axle out from the non-drive side. Be careful not to dislodge the ball bearings.

• Clean the cones and axle and inspect them for damage. Check to see if the axle is bent by rolling it on a flat surface and looking for irregular motion. Replace damaged cones or bent axles immediately.

• Remove the bearings and clean with degreaser. Replace any that have scores or flat spots on their surface. Reinsert and pack with grease (*inset*).

Insert an Allen key into the 8mm or 10mm Allen bolt located in the centre of the freehub. This bolt holds the freehub body on to the axle.

• Turn the key anti-clockwise to remove the freehub. You may need a bit of force to loosen this bolt so use an Allen key with a long handle for extra leverage.

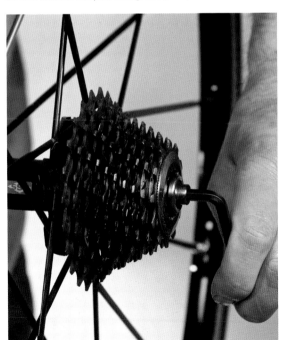

Mavic wheels, as well as some made by other manufacturers, have a simple way of taking up any slack and wear in the bearings.

• Remove the wheel from the bike, as well as the quick-release skewer from the hub axle.

• The inside ends of the axle are shaped to receive an Allen key. Place an Allen key in each end of the axle and tighten the cones. Tighten only enough to take up any slack – do not over-tighten as this can damage the bearings.

WHEELS

Quick-release mechanisms help to remove and replace a wheel quicker than ever before. The tyres are the component that make contact with the ground. Match the tyres on your bike to the prevailing riding conditions and always be ready to replace worn-out tyres.

Quick-release wheels

Removing and refitting a wheel is a straightforward task, but if any of the following steps are overlooked, the wheel may come loose and compromise the rider's safety. The steps are for wheels with quick-release levers that secure them in the drop-outs (the recess in the frame into which the axle fits). For bikes with axle nuts, loosening and tightening with a spanner corresponds to unlocking and locking the quick-release lever.

Levers are labelled "locked" or "closed" on the side facing the cyclist when the wheel is secure, and "unlocked" or "open" when it is not. Check levers are locked before each ride, and during a ride if disc brakes are fitted.

The rim brake needs to be released on the wheel being removed. For V-brakes, unhook the cable from its cradle; for cantilevers unhook the straddle wire from the left brake arm; for callipers, use the quick-release lever.

STEP LOCATOR

Parts of the quick-release system

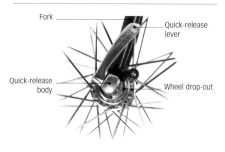

Fork

Quick-release lever

Quick-release body

Wheel drop-out

Toolbox

• Spanners for wheels with axle nuts

Removing a rear wheel

1 Release the brake, shift the chain on to the smallest sprocket and pull the quick-release lever away from the bike into the unlocked position. Some quick-release levers are shaped so that they bend towards the frame when in the locked position. This provides a visual check if nothing is printed on the lever.

Removing a front wheel

1 **Release the brake**. Pull the quick-release lever to the unlocked position. If the drop-out has safety lips, the wheel will not come out of the fork at this stage. These safety lips prevent the wheel falling out in the unlikely event of the lever becoming unlocked while you ride.

● Use your fingers to unscrew the nut on the opposite side of the lever until the quick-release clears the safety lip.

2 **Lift up the bike** to allow the wheel to drop out of the fork.

● Replace the front wheel by reversing Step 1.

● Push the quick-release lever behind the left fork leg to prevent anything catching it and opening it accidentally.

● Reconnect the brake once the wheel is locked.

2 **Hook the chain** out of the way and on to the peg situated on the inner side of the right seat stay (if there is one).

● Pull the rear mech back and then lift up the rear of the bike.

● Give the tyre a sharp blow from above with the heel of your hand if the wheel does not drop forwards and out of the frame.

3 **Replace the wheel** by introducing the hub axle to the drop-outs.

● Hook the chain on to the smallest sprocket, then push or pull the wheel backwards.

● Line up the tyre exactly in the middle of the chainstays as you hold the wheel straight.

● Push the quick-release lever into the locked position to secure the wheel. Reconnect the brake.

Puncture repair

When you are out on a ride, it is much easier to replace a punctured inner tube with an intact tube rather than painstakingly mend the puncture. At home, you can repair the punctured tube with adhesive and a patch. It is still a good idea to carry a repair kit on every ride, because you might be unlucky enough to get a second puncture and be forced to repair the tube outdoors.

The main point to remember about mending a puncture is not to rush any of the stages. If you patiently give the glue time to dry, closely examine the inside of the tyre, and carefully refit the tube, then you will be rewarded with a successful repair. If you miss anything or trap the inner tube, you may get another puncture.

STEP LOCATOR

Parts of a wheel

Tyre   Inner tube   Valve   Rim

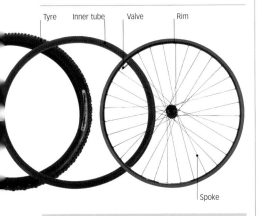

Spoke

Toolbox

● Tyre levers ● Crayon ● Sandpaper ● Chalk
● Patch adhesive ● Repair patches

Mending a punctured inner tube

1 **Take the wheel out** of the bike. Place one tyre lever under the tyre bead and lift it off the rim. Hook this lever around one of the spokes.

● Insert another lever under the tyre near to the hooked lever. Push the second lever forwards and run it around the whole circumference of the rim to remove one side of the tyre.

● Remove the inner tube from the rim.

4 **Take the tyre off the wheel,** turn it inside out and thoroughly check the inner surface.

● Remove anything that is sticking through the tyre by pulling it out from the outside of the tyre.

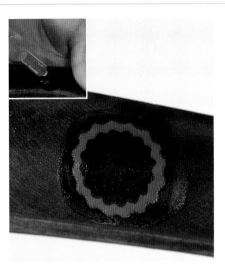

2 **Inflate the tube** a little and listen for the sound of escaping air. Locate the hole, mark it with a crayon, and let the air out of the tube.

• Spread a thin layer of adhesive over and around the hole (*inset*). Allow time for it to become tacky.

• Peel the foil from the patch. Press the patch firmly on to the adhesive for over a minute. Make sure that the edges are flat.

3 **Use a small piece of sandpaper** to dust some chalk over the patch to prevent excess adhesive from sticking to the inside of the tyre.

• Leave the tube for a few minutes to make sure that the adhesive has dried

5 **Put one side of the tyre** fully back on to the rim. Slightly inflate the tube, insert the valve into the hole in the rim, and then work the tube back inside the tyre.

• Put the other side of the tyre in place by pushing the valve upwards, then lifting the section of tyre next to the valve over the rim. Work the tyre back around the rim.

• Check that the tyre has not trapped the tube underneath it before fully inflating the tube. To do this, pinch the tyre together and look around the whole circumference of the wheel.

Spokes and rims

The steps in this sequence explain how to replace a single broken spoke and how to true a wheel, a term for straightening the rim of a wheel. However, replacing multiple spokes, replacing spokes in non-standard wheels, and truing a wheel that has been buckled by some kind of impact are jobs that are best left to the experts in a good bike repair shop.

It is essential to true the wheel after replacing a broken spoke because the wheel rim is kept straight by the combined pull of all the spokes acting on it. If one spoke breaks, its pull is missed and the rim as a whole goes out of line.

A wheel jig is needed to true a wheel properly. This tool holds the wheel securely in place and its jaws provide a reference point either side of the rim to help judge how out of line the wheel has become. Bringing it in line is a matter of tightening the new spoke until it reaches the same tension as the old spoke.

STEP LOCATOR

Parts of a spoke

Spoke head
Spoke
Bend
Nipple head · Nipple · Threads · Spoke

Toolbox
- Spoke key • Wheel jig
- Long-nosed pliers

Replacing a spoke and truing a wheel

1 **Remove the wheel** and take off the tyre and inner tube.

● Lift up the rim tape next to the broken spoke and push the spoke upwards and out of the rim. If the head of the spoke is broken, measure the broken spoke so you can buy the correct length to replace it. If the break occurred in another place, measure the two pieces to get the right length.

4 **Screw the nipple** on to the spoke. For the first few turns you can use your fingers.

● Go back to Step 2 and check that it is laced exactly the same way as the spoke four along from it. If it is not laced properly, tensioning the spoke in Steps 5 and 6 could damage the wheel.

Insert the new spoke, threads first, into the hub flange from the opposite side to its two neighbours.

● Lace the new spoke into the wheel, under and over the neighbouring spokes. To do this, look at the spoke four along and lace the new spoke exactly the same way.

Push the nipple of the new spoke through the rim hole from inside the rim and screw it on to the spoke.

● Remove the rim tape to make it easier to fit the nipple on to the new spoke.

● Check the rim tape – if you see any splits, or if it is frayed, replace the tape.

Put the wheel into a wheel jig and take up the remaining slack on the spoke nipple by tightening it with a spoke key. Make sure that the spoke key is precisely the right size for the nipples on the wheel.

● Stop short of making the spoke as tight as its neighbours at this stage.

Use small, measured turns of the spoke key to tension the spoke.

● Rotate the wheel so that the nipple of the new spoke is between the jaws of your jig.

● Note how out of line the rim is, then give the nipple a one-quarter tightening turn and check again between the jaws. Repeat and check each quarter turn until the rim is straight.

ADJUSTING YOUR BRAKES

Trustworthy brakes are a bike's most important component. The braking system needs to be adjusted and serviced with careful precision to guarantee a rider's safety in all conditions.

RIM BRAKES

*Rim brakes stop a bike by contacting the rim of the wheels.
Pads must be checked to ensure that they contact the rim
fully and at the same time, and replaced when they are worn.
Brake cables must be checked and lubricated regularly.*

How they work

The three most common types of rim brake, V-brake,
cantilever, and calliper, work in a similar way. A lever
pulls a cable, which causes the two brake arms to
move towards each other simultaneously. This action
brings the two pads into contact with the braking
surface of the wheel rim. Springs cause the arms to
move back when the lever is released. Cantilever
brakes distribute the cable's pull via a straddle wire.
The inner cable in a V-brake and calliper pulls one
arm, while the outer, in resisting this pull, effectively
pushes the other arm.

Braking safely
Rim brakes must be set up
properly and maintained to
very high standards if they
are to work effectively and
safely on any surface and in
all conditions.

V-BRAKE ANATOMY

The cable of a V-brake is attached to a brake
arm by a cable-clamp bolt. When pulled, the
cable pulls this arm towards the rim. At the
same time, the cable-guide tube, which is an
extension of the cable outer, pushes the other
arm inwards. The two arms pivot around the
brake bosses, pushing the brake pads against
the braking surface on the rim. Once the cable's
pull is released, springs around the pivot bolts
push both brake arms apart.

Cable-guide tube
*Pushes the brake
arm*

Brake arm
*Pivots inwards on
a brake boss*

Inner cable
*Pulls the
brake arm*

Cable-clamp bolt
Attaches the cable to the brake arm

Brake boss
Allows the brake arm to pivot

Brake pad
*Contacts the rim and stops
the wheel*

Springs
Push brake arms apart

Pivot bolt
*Anchors the
brake arm to
the brake boss*

Brake lever
Pulls the cable

Brake arm
Moves the brake pads towards the rim

Brake pad
Slows down the wheel

BRAKE LEVER ANATOMY

When the rider applies the brake lever it pulls the nipple of the inner cable. As it leaves the lever, the brake cable runs inside a cable outer, which sits in a barrel adjuster. This barrel adjuster allows the brake travel to be fine-tuned.

Nipple
Fixes inner cable to brake lever

Brake lever
Pulls the nipple

Inner cable
Links the brake arm to the brake lever

Barrel adjuster
Adjusts brake travel

Cable outer
Resists the pull on the cable

Drop handlebar brake cable

Brake cables on a drop handlebar need to be changed at regular intervals, although this depends on how much the road bike is used. For a heavily used bike, change the brake cables every two months; for a bike ridden lightly two or three times a week, change the brake cables once a year.

The steps in this sequence are performed on the back brake. Replacing a cable on the front brake follows the same principles, but there are no cable guides to thread through.

Brake levers that fit a drop handlebar require a brake cable with a pear nipple. Always keep a new cable in the toolbox or workshop as a spare. A rear cable can be cut to fit the front as well. Once the cable has been removed, remember to put a few drops of lubricant on the pivots around which the brake lever moves, and spray some oil into the tube inside the lever hood where the cable is inserted.

STEP LOCATOR

Parts of a brake lever and brake cable

Brake lever hood
Brake cable
Pear-shaped nipple
Brake lever
Brake cable
Campagnolo Ergoshift

Toolbox

- Long-nosed pliers ● Cable cutters
- Allen key multi-tool ● Fine round file

Replacing road bike brake cables

1 **Loosen the cable-clamp bolt** on the brake calliper. Remove the old cable by pulling its nipple from the lever hood with long-nosed pliers.

● Note exactly where the cable fits in the lever hood to allow you to fit the new one easily.

● If the old cable has broken, remove the part of the cable that is still clamped to the calliper.

● Carefully unwind the handlebar tape.

4 **Fit each length** of cable outer with a metal ferrule at both ends. When you apply the brake, ferrules prevent the cable outers from being pulled through the cable guides on the frame.

● Make sure that each ferrule is fully pushed home. Put a little oil on the end of the ferrule to help it slide into place and wipe off any excess.

Insert the new, greased cable into the cradle on the lever in which the nipple sits.

● Thread the cable into the tube in the lever hood. Push it in and look for it coming out of the back of the lever hood. Now pull it through the lever hood from behind.

● Make sure that the nipple is seated in the brake lever cradle when the cable is all the way through.

Cut the new cable outer to length with good-quality cable cutters. Measure the old outer and cut the new one to the same length.

● Always cut between the spirals of the cable outer.

● Dribble oil into the cable outer, holding it while the oil runs down to coat the inside.

● Renew cable outers at regular intervals.

Thread the cable through the first length of cable outer and the first cable guide.

● Pull the cable all the way through and insert it into the next guide, then the next outer.

● Push the cable outers firmly into the guides, to ensure there is no slack when applying the brakes.

● Use a fine round file to file out any tight cable guides. Do not file more than you have to.

Pull the cable through the cable-clamp bolt on the calliper until each brake pad is about 2mm from the wheel rim.

● Hold the cable and tighten the clamp bolt. If the brake has a quick release, ensure that it is in the closed position before tightening the clamp bolt.

● Follow Steps 5 and 6 on p.107 to re-tape the handlebar, with either new or existing tape.

Straight handlebar brake cable

Replacing the brake cable inners and outers is a job that should be done fairly often on a mountain bike – about once every six to 12 months. They also need replacing if they start fraying and become worn. The hybrid bike in this sequence has V-brakes, but some mountain bikes are equipped with cantilever brakes. Fitting cables is similar for both.

Brake cables also require regular cleaning and lubricating, especially if the bike has been ridden consistently in wet weather. All brake levers that fit on to a straight or riser handlebar require a cable with a barrel nipple.

Regardless of the manufacturer, the barrel nipple fits into the brake lever in the same way. Remember to use ferrules on both ends of every length of new outer cable. Crimp a cable tidy on the end of the cable, once everything is secure and working as it should.

In these steps the tyre is removed from the wheel to show clearly what is happening.

STEP LOCATOR

Parts of a brake lever and a brake cable

Brake lever — Ring clamp — Reach adjuster — Brake lever — Barrel adjuster

Brake cable — Nipple — Brake cable

Toolbox

- Long-nosed pliers ● Cable cutters
- Allen key multi-tool ● Cable pullers (optional)

Replacing V-brake cables on a hybrid bike

1 **Undo the cable-clamp bolt** on the brake. Note where the nipple sits in the cradle that is part of the lever and remove the cable from inside the brake lever by pulling it out with long-nosed pliers.

● Check the outer cables. If they are not worn, you can use them again. Flush them out with degreaser and dribble oil into them.

4 **Attach the cable** to the brake arm by inserting it in the cable guide tube and then pull it through the cable-clamp bolt.

● Keep the cable under tension and check that each length of cable outer is properly seated in the cable guides.

● Pull the cable to bring the brake pads closer to the rim. Tighten the clamp bolt when the pads are about 2mm from the rim.

2 **Cut new cable outers** to the same length as the outers you removed or measure them up on your bike and trim as needed. Buy cable outer either in a roll or in pre-cut lengths with inners in a cable kit. The pre-cut lengths may be too long for your bike so you may still have to cut to fit.

● Dribble oil into each cable outer and push a metal ferrule on to each end.

3 **Grease the new inner** and thread it into the brake lever. When it shows through the barrel adjuster, pull it from this side of the lever until the nipple is seated in the lever cradle.

● Thread the cable through the lengths of cable outer and seat the cable outers in the cable guides of the frame.

5 **Pull the brake lever** until the brake is fully applied. This ensures that all cable outers are bedded in and all bolts are tight.

● Undo the cable-clamp bolt and repeat Step 4 if the cable slips through the clamp bolt or a ferrule is not seated properly.

6 **Cut off any excess cable** once the cables are bedded in.

● Leave about 4cm (1½in) of free cable after the cable-clamp bolt.

● Crimp a cable tidy on the end of the cable to prevent it from fraying.

Calliper brake

Maintaining calliper brakes is a question of regularly checking the action of the brake lever. If you have to pull it too far before the brake bites, the brake needs adjusting. Check the brake pads for wear and alignment, and ensure that they contact the braking surface of the rims simultaneously.

How far the lever has to be pulled before the brake comes on depends on the rider. People with smaller hands may prefer more travel in the lever before the brake bites, because they will pull with more strength the closer the lever is to the handlebar.

Apart from their quick releases, all dual-pivot calliper brakes (such as the Shimano brakes shown here) work in the same way, regardless of the manufacturer. This means that you should be able to apply these steps to your bike, whatever its brakes.

STEP LOCATOR

Parts of a calliper brake

Travel adjuster, spring, and washer

Calliper arm

Centre-fixing bolt

Centring adjusting screw

Brake shoe bolt

Brake pad

Brake shoe

ULTEGRA

Toolbox
- Full set of Allen keys or Allen key multi-tool
- Long-nosed pliers (optional)

Adjusting a calliper brake

1 **Periodically check for pad wear**. If the pads are wearing down towards half their original depth they must be replaced.

● Undo the Allen key pad retainer and push out the pad. If the pad and shoe are a complete piece, replace the whole unit, releasing the old pad and fitting the new one with a 5mm Allen key.

3 **Pull the brake on** with the brake lever and check to see if both pads simultaneously come into contact with the braking surface on the rim of the wheel.

● Make sure that both sides are working together by turning an adjustment screw on the side of the calliper with an Allen key. This process is called "centring" the brakes.

Using quick-release mechanisms

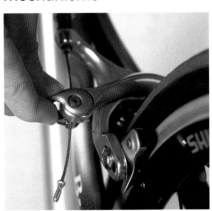

2 **Adjust the brake pads** so they are directly in line with the braking surface of the rim.

● Release the 5mm Allen bolt on the pad and line the pad up with the braking surface.

● Look for pad wear at this point. Pads that have been set too low will develop a lip and will need to be replaced.

1 **Use a quick-release mechanism** when the adjusted brake pads are so close to the rim that it is impossible to remove the wheel. Campagnolo and Shimano calliper brakes are equipped with different quick-release systems.

● Lift the small lever on the cable-fixing bolt to make Shimano calliper brake pads move away from the rim. After replacing the wheel, lower the lever.

4 **Adjust the brake travel** if you have to pull the brake lever back a long way towards the handlebar before the wheel stops moving.

● Undo the cable-fixing bolt and squeeze the sides of the calliper until the pads nearly touch the rim. The brake cable will then move through the fixing bolt.

● Tighten the bolt and release the calliper.

1 **Press the small button** at the side of the brake lever to move Campagnolo calliper brake pads away from the rim.

● Restore the pads to their original position by pulling the brake lever towards the handlebar until the brakes are on and then push the small button back.

V-brake

V-brakes are fitted to most new mountain bikes because they give good stopping power. Maintaining brake performance is crucial because of the harsh conditions to which mountain bikes are sometimes subjected, so knowing how to adjust the brakes at home and out on the trail is very important.

Pad alignment and brake travel need to be checked and adjusted regularly to keep them working properly. Bear in mind that as soon as you ride off-road you will increase brake pad wear. Even a single ride can render already worn pads useless, so change them before they need it.

Adjustment in the workshop, especially pad alignment, is best performed with the tyre removed, since off-road tyres are bulky and can be in the way. Wheels must run true before setting up brakes (*see pp.118–19*).

STEP LOCATOR

Parts of a V-brake

Cradle

V-brake arm

Spring clip

Spacers

Cable-fixing bolt

Pivot bolt

Brake shoe

Brake pad

Toolbox
- Full set of Allen keys or Allen key multi-tool
- Cross-head screwdriver • Cable puller (optional)

Adjusting a V-brake

1 **Check that the stopper** pin on each brake arm is seated in the same hole on the brake bosses. If it is not, remove the pivot bolt, slide the brake arm off the boss, and put the pin into the correct hole.

- Replace the pivot bolt and re-tighten it. If you notice that the brake boss was dry with the arm removed, smear a little grease on it.

4 **Re-tension the brakes** by hooking the cable back in its cradle.

- Check that the gap between each brake pad and the rim of the wheel is 1mm.

- Undo the cable-fixing bolt with an Allen key and pull the cable through until the 1mm gap is achieved. Then tighten the cable-fixing bolt.

2 **Press the brake arms together.** If they are not vertical when the pads touch the rim, rearrange the spacers either side of the pads until they are vertical.

● Release the brakes by unhooking the cable-guide tube from the cradle. Do this when you remove the wheel with correctly adjusted V-brakes.

3 **Undo the brake-pad** fixing bolt, remove the pad and shoe assembly, and swap the spacers around.

● Check the pads. If they are worn, remove the pad-retaining clip, push the old pad from the shoe, and replace it with a new one.

● Line up the pads so that they hit the rim with their entire braking surface, and are parallel to it. Then tighten the fixing bolts.

5 **Use a cross-head screwdriver** to tighten or loosen the centring screw on each brake arm. The aim is to make both arms move an equal distance before the pad touches the rim when you apply the brake lever.

● The tension on each screw should ideally be even, since there is an equal number of spacers on either side of the brake arm.

6 **Screw out the barrel adjuster** on the brake lever to reduce brake travel and make the brakes feel more responsive.

● Screw the adjuster outwards to reduce brake travel and create firmer braking. This technique is quick and easy to perform, and is especially useful for riding in the wet when brake pads can wear down rapidly.

Cantilever brake

Cantilever brakes work with the brake levers that fit dropped handlebars, whereas V-brakes do not. This is why touring and cyclo-cross bikes are fitted with cantilevers. Cantilevers were the predecessors of V-brakes, so they may also be fitted to older mountain and hybrid bikes.

Keep cantilever brakes running smoothly by regularly checking the pads for wear and adjusting the pad alignment and brake travel.

The cable of the cantilever brake shown in these steps is clamped to one brake arm and the straddle wire running off it attaches to the other arm. On some older cantilever brakes, the brake cable is attached to a straddle. This hooks the straddle wire that transfers the cable's pull to both brake arms and needs regular adjustment (*see Step 1 Adjusting a BMX U-brake, pp.134–5*).

STEP LOCATOR

Parts of a cantilever brake

Brake shoe · Brake pad
Cantilever arm · Cable-clamp bolt
Spring clip
Brake pad Allen nut · Spacers

Toolbox

- 5mm Allen key • Grease gun (optional)
- Grease

Adjusting a cantilever brake

1 **Disconnect the straddle wire** by pushing the cantilever arm to which it is attached towards the wheel with one hand. At the same time, unhook the nipple on the straddle with the other hand.

- Undo the pivot bolts that attach the cantilever arms to the frame bosses.
- Remove the cantilever arms.

1 mm

2 mm

4 **Angle the pads** so that the front of each pad hits the rim before the rear when the brakes are applied – this is called "toe in".

- Loosen the pad-fixing bolt and place a cosmetic emery board between the rear of the pad and the rim. Apply the brakes and then tighten the bolt. Release the brakes and remove the emery board. Ideally, the front of the pad should be 1mm from the rim and the rear 2mm.

2 **Clean the exposed frame bosses** with a cloth soaked in degreaser, then lubricate with a light grease, not a heavy-duty industrial grease. Use a grease gun if you have one.

● Bolt both arms back on to the bosses, making sure that the stopper pins are inserted into the same hole on each boss.

● Replace the pivot bolts and then tighten them to hold the brake arms to the bosses.

3 **Check the pads.** If one is worn or badly aligned, undo the pad-fixing bolt with an Allen key and remove the pad/shoe assembly.

● Remove the spring clip from the brake shoe and slide out the worn pad. Slide in a new pad and replace the spring clip.

● Return the assembly to the brake arm, line up the pad so that its entire surface contacts the rim, and is parallel with it, then tighten the bolt.

5 **Undo the brake-cable clamp** to achieve the proper spacing from the pad to the rim.

● Pull the cable through the clamp until the front of each brake pad is 1mm from the rim. Tighten the clamp bolt.

● Pull the brake lever to see if both brake arms contact the rim simultaneously. If they do not, screw the centring screws in or out on each arm until they do.

Alternative brake designs

Two alternative brake designs are commonly fitted to some new bikes. These are the side-pull calliper brakes used on children's bikes and the U-brakes fitted on BMX bikes. Side-pulls work in much the same way as callipers (see pp.128–9), while U-brakes resemble cantilevers (see pp.132–3).

Before buying replacement cables for either of these types of brake, first check the kind of nipple that is presently used on the bike in question. Some levers on children's bikes and older bikes require pear nipples, while other levers need barrel nipples. When a new cable is fitted to a side-pull calliper brake, leave the barrel adjuster at the halfway point of its range.

STEP LOCATOR

Parts of a side-pull brake and a U-brake

Side-pull calliper brake

- Barrel adjuster
- Pivot nut
- Brake arms
- Cable-clamp bolt
- Brake pad
- Brake-pad bolt

BMX U-brake

- Brake arms
- Straddle-wire seat
- Centring screw
- Straddle-clamp bolt
- Pivot bolts
- Brake-pad bolt
- Brake pads

Toolbox

- Allen key multi-tool ● Long-nosed pliers
- Spanners

Adjusting a side-pull calliper brake

1 **Loosen the cable–clamp bolt** and pull the cable through until the brake pads are closer to the rim. This compensates for pad wear.

● Screw in the barrel adjuster to move the pads away or screw it out to move them closer.

● Replace pads that are worn below half their depth by undoing the pad bolt and fitting a new pad or shoe unit in their place.

Adjusting a BMX U-brake

1 **Undo the straddle clamp** bolt and pull the brake cable through the straddle with long-nosed pliers to take up the pad wear. Then tighten the nut.

2 **Use an Allen key** to adjust the centring screw on each brake arm if the pads do not contact the rim at the same time. Screw in to move the pad away from the rim.

Centre the brakes if one brake pad is contacting the rim before the other.

• Undo the brake's pivot nut that holds it in place and is located behind the fork crown.

• Hold the calliper so that both pads are an equal distance from the rim and tighten the pivot nut.

Undo the pad bolts, line up the pads and tighten the bolt so that the brake pads contact the rim directly in line with it. Do this when you replace worn pads, too.

• Inspect the pads regularly. If you find any ridges on them, replace the pads (see *Step 1*) and then line them up as described above, so that the whole of their surface contacts the rim.

Line up or replace pads in the same way as calliper brakes (see *pp. 128–9*). Replace the brake pads by removing the pad bolts and fitting new pad and shoe units.

• To disconnect the brake, pinch the brake arms together and unhook the straddle from the straddle wire. To reconnect, reverse this procedure.

HUB-MOUNTED BRAKES

Hub-mounted brakes stop a bike by slowing down the speed of the hub. Regularly check disc brake pads for wear and alignment, replacing them when they are worn. Regularly check and replace the cables on cable discs and hub brakes. Examine the hoses of hydraulic brakes for leaks.

How they work

Hub-mounted brakes are activated by the pull of a lever on a cable, which causes pads to contact a braking surface. Springs push the pads away when the lever is released. In disc brakes, the pads act on discs attached to the hub.

    In roller and coaster brakes, the pads act on a braking surface inside the hub. The action of the pads on the surface then slows down the hub and therefore the wheel. In hydraulic brakes, the lever's action pushes fluid through a hose; this fluid pushes the brake pads in the calliper into action. Of all the hub-mounted brakes, hydraulic disc brakes offer a rider the best control over the braking forces that can be applied.

Working in all weathers
An advantage of hub brakes over rim brakes is that their performance is largely unaffected by adverse riding conditions.

HYDRAULIC DISC BRAKE ANATOMY

When the rider pulls the brake lever, the hydraulic fluid in the hose pushes on the pistons in the calliper. These pistons in turn cause the brake pad on each side of the disc to contact the disc and to slow the rotation of the wheel. When the rider releases the brake lever, the pressure of the fluid in the hose decreases, allowing the springs (not visible) in the calliper to push the brake pads apart.

Hose
Contains fluid

Calliper
Contains pistons and two brake pads

Brake pad
Contacts the disc under pressure from the fluid

Disc
Slows down the hub of the wheel under pressure from the brake pads

Hose
Carries the brake fluid from the lever to the calliper

Brake lever
Compresses the brake fluid

HYDRAULIC BRAKE LEVER

Brake hoses are connected to a reservoir of brake fluid on each brake lever. The fluid fills the hoses all the way to the calliper on the wheel. Pulling the brake lever operates a piston in the reservoir, which pushes the fluid down the hose and, as a result, activates the calliper pistons.

Calliper
Houses the braking mechanism

Disc
Slows down the wheel

Replacing disc brake pads

When brake pads wear down, the brakes will not stop the wheel as quickly. Eventually, the pads become so worn that they have to be replaced. Unevenly worn pads should also be replaced immediately and the calliper may need to be realigned (see p.141).

Although replacing pads is broadly the same for all makes and models of disc brake, there are some differences, mostly in the way the pads are retained within the brake calliper. Some brake pads are kept in position within the calliper by retaining bolts, while others rely on the spring that keeps the two pads apart to fix them in place.

Only use replacement pads recommended by the manufacturer of your brakes, and be very careful how you handle the pads.

STEP LOCATOR

Parts of a disc-brake calliper

Brake hose

Calliper

Rotor

Brake pads (not visible)

Toolbox
- Allen or Torx keys
- Flat-bladed screwdriver

Changing the pads

1 **Remove the wheel from the frame** or forks (see pp.140-1), depending on which brake you are working on.

- Taking care not to touch the disc brake rotor, lower the wheel from the bike by supporting it with both hands on the axle, either side of the hub.
- If you do touch a rotor you must clean it, or the performance of the brake will be reduced (see pp.126-7).

4 **Place the new pads on either side** of the spring, which is V-shaped when looked at from the side. The tabs of the pads should be at the open end of the V. The narrowest part of the V goes into the calliper first.

- Taking care not to touch the pad surface, hold the pad and spring assembly between the thumb and forefinger, ready to put it in the calliper.

2 **Remove the pad from the calliper.** The pads on this model are held in place within the calliper by outward pressure from a spring.

• Before you can push the pads out, you need to prise them apart with a flat-bladed screwdriver.

• If your brakes have a mechanism for taking up pad wear you need to fully wind it out.

• If your bike has a pad-retaining bolt, remove it with an Allen key.

3 **Once the pads are dislodged,** and all internal pressure is off them, squeeze them together. Use the tabs at the front of the pads to pull them free from the calliper. Sometimes they need a gentle push from behind with a flat-bladed screwdriver.

• If you have to push them, take each pad out separately and ensure that the separating spring comes out, too.

5 **Squeeze the pad/spring assembly** together and push it into the open end of the calliper. Slide the assembly all the way in, listening for the "click" sound that indicates it is seated correctly in the calliper. Let go once you hear the "click".

• The pads should separate when you let go of them. If they don't, remove and reassemble them, then push them in again, repeating Steps 2–5.

6 **Put the wheel back in the frame** or fork, ensuring the quick-release lever is locked.

• Bed the pads in by spinning the wheel and pulling the brake lever a number of times. Ride the bike for a short time to test the brakes fully.

• Some brakes have micro-adjusters for fine-tuning their action – adjust this feature if present on your brakes.

Disc-brake care

Cable disc brakes work well in all conditions. Even so, check the brake cables regularly for signs of fraying and keep them well lubricated. If the brakes do not release quickly when you let go of the brake lever, they need lubricating. Check brake travel, too, since excessive travel can mean that the brake pads are worn.

When lubricating your bike, make sure that the lubricant does not fall on or touch the brake discs or pads. Do not even touch the disc or pad faces, because the grease from your fingers can easily affect their performance. Always clean the discs with a specialist rotor-cleaning fluid.

Check your disc brake rotors regularly for trueness and cracks, and clean them after every ride to ensure good brake performance. Replace a cracked or buckled rotor at once.

STEP LOCATOR

Parts of a cable disc brake (front)

- Cable outer
- Brake cable
- Brake calliper
- Hub
- Brake disc
- Rotor-mounting bolts

Toolbox

- Allen or Torx keys ● Long-nosed pliers
- Rotor cleaner ● Clean cloth

Adjusting cable travel

1 **Loosen the cable–clamp bolt** on the calliper and pull through enough cable, with pliers or a cable-pulling tool, to take up any slack in the cable.

● Tighten the clamp bolt. This will reduce the travel on the brakes and is a necessary adjustment if the brake levers need pulling a long way before the brakes work.

Looking after rotors

1 **Check the rotor for trueness** by inspecting how it moves through the calliper when the wheel is turned. It should run absolutely straight and true.

● Spin the wheel quite quickly, but ensure you are holding your bike steady.

Screw out the barrel adjuster to reduce brake travel. The adjuster is just above where the cable outer sits on the calliper body.

● Loosen the fixing clamp to remove the old cable if a new cable is needed. Insert the new cable into the brake lever (see pp.126–7) and follow Steps 1 and 2 with the new cable.

● Lubricate the new cable before you fit it.

Align the callipers with the discs using the adjustment bolts. Undo these bolts, align the calliper so that its sides are parallel with the disc, and then tighten.

● Align brakes that are not equipped with this adjustment facility by using spacers to pack out the calliper-fixing bolts.

Remove a cracked or buckled rotor by unscrewing the bolts holding it to the hub with an Allen or Torx key. Replace it with the specific rotor for your type of brake.

● Place the new rotor over the threaded bolt holes in the hub. Screw in and tighten the bolts.

Clean the rotor with a specialist rotor-cleaning fluid after removing the wheel.

● Spray a little cleaner on either side of the rotor.

● Use a clean cloth to prevent the cleaner coating other bike parts but also to ensure the rotor is covered with cleaner. Do not polish with it.

Hydraulic disc brake I

Hydraulic disc brakes are more powerful than cable disc brakes, and once correctly installed, will require less maintenance. A bike that has disc-brake mountings on the frame and fork will be suitable for fitting a disc-brake system to.

Cable disc brakes can work with rim-brake levers but their performance falls fractionally short of hydraulic systems. These work by compressing a fluid rather than pulling a cable. Compatible hydraulic brake levers will need to be fitted to the handlebar and brake hoses that hold the brake fluid. Disc-specific hubs will also be required.

There is no need to fasten the front hose to the fork. To direct and keep the rear hose in place, use an adaptor kit to let the frame's cable guides take hoses, because the cable hole in a standard cable guide is too small.

STEP LOCATOR

Parts of a hydraulic disc brake

- Calliper
- Hose
- Wheel quick release
- Disc bolt
- Disc

Toolbox

- Allen or Torx keys • Spanner • Stanley knife
- Thread-locking compound • Flat screwdriver

Installing a hydraulic disc-brake system

1 **Fit the calliper** using the Allen bolts and washers provided.

● Swap the washers around to pack out each calliper in order to line it up with the disc.

● Apply a thread-locking compound to the threads, then fix the disc to the hub using the disc bolts.

2 **Cut the hose** of the hydraulic system if it is too long by following Steps 3–7.

• Take out the brake pads (*see pp.138–9*) first and replace them with a spacer. The calliper used here is a demonstration model with no hose attached.

3 **Mount the brake lever** on to the handlebar and secure with the clamp bolts.

• Unscrew the aluminium shroud located where the hose joins the brake lever and move it out of the way. Prise open the brass olive beneath with a flat screwdriver.

4 **Move the brass olive** along the hose and out of the way.

• Prise the hose off the brake lever joint with a flat screwdriver, but be careful not to damage the lever joint. At the same time, gently pull on the hose to detach it.

5 **Carefully cut off** excess cable from the detached end of the hose with a sharp knife. Keep the olive and the shroud on the part of the hose that you will be reconnecting.

6 **Join the hose** to the brake lever by inserting it on to the lever joint. Push it home firmly, but not too hard as this can split the hose.

• Hold the hose upwards as you work to keep brake fluid loss to a minimum.

7 **Squeeze the olive** on to the hose at the lever joint to make a good seal.

• Screw the shroud on to the thread of the lever joint.

• Bleed the disc-brake system (*see pp.144–5*).

Hydraulic disc brake II

If you are pulling hard on the brake levers without much effect on the discs, or if you are pulling the levers several times to make the brakes work, you need to bleed air from the system. The following steps will also help if you have cut hoses to fit while installing a hydraulic system, had a leak in the system, or have fitted a new hose.

STEP LOCATOR

Toolbox
- Allen key multi-tool • 10mm spanner
- Length of clear hose

4 **Angle the bike** so that the reservoir is level, open the bleed nipple and fill the reservoir with brake fluid. Pour with a smooth, constant stream to minimize air bubbles.

- Squeeze the brake lever all the way to the handlebar and hold it. Close the bleed nipple.

- Never mix brake fluids. Mineral oil or DOT 4 fluids cannot be interchanged.

Draining and replacing brake fluid

1 **Remove the wheels** from the bike to reduce the chance of brake fluid falling on the brake discs.

- Place a spacer in the calliper between the brake pads (see Step 2, p.143).

- Take off the brake fluid reservoir cover on the brake lever with an Allen key. Be careful not to let any of the brake fluid touch your hands.

5 **Repeat Step 4,** filling up the reservoir until there are no more air bubbles flowing through the clear tube when you squeeze the brake lever. You will probably have to repeat this step four or five times before the bubbles in the tube completely disappear.

- Close the bleed nipple once the tube is bubble-free and the reservoir is full.

Open the bleed nipple on the calliper with a 10mm spanner.

• Slide one end of a short length of clear tube on to the bleed nipple.

• Put the other end of the tube into a plastic container that is big enough to collect the old brake fluid.

Pull the brake lever all the way back to the handlebar to remove some brake fluid.

• Tighten the bleed nipple.

• Make sure that all tools are to hand since the next steps require you to be organized.

• Cover the surface below where you are working since brake fluids can be corrosive. Use disposable mechanic's gloves to protect your hands.

Replace the cover of the brake fluid reservoir but be careful not to displace any brake fluid.

• Refit your wheels and pump the brake lever a few times to centre the brake pads.

• Go for a flat test ride. If your brakes are not performing as they should there may still be air in the system. Repeat Step 4 and make sure that everything is tight.

Roller-brake cable

All brake cables wear out, no matter how much time is spent maintaining them. Cables for roller brakes – sometimes called drum brakes – are no different. If the bike is equipped with roller brakes, the steps in this sequence show how to replace a cable when it is frayed or worn out. However, lubricating the brakes and replacing the internal parts are occasional jobs that are best left to the experts at a good bike shop.

If the rear inner tube is punctured, or it is necessary to take off the back tyre to replace it, you need to know how to disconnect the rear brake in order to remove the back wheel. At the same time, you should know how to reconnect and adjust the brake after replacing the wheel. Once this is a familiar routine, it will also be possible to adjust the roller brakes for brake pad wear from time to time.

STEP LOCATOR

Parts of a roller brake

Brake body

Wheel axle nut

Brake arm

Cable-clamp bolt

Barrel adjuster | Cable guide | Cable

Toolbox

- Spanners
- Long-nosed pliers

Replacing a roller-brake cable

1 **Push the brake-arm cradle** towards the front of the bike. This takes the tension from the cable so that you can unhook the cable-clamp bolt from the cradle and remove the old cable.

- Screw the barrel adjuster on the brake arm in or out to about half of its extent.

- Remove the wheel at this point if you need to replace the tyre or inner tube.

4 **Tighten the cable-clamp bolt** while squeezing the cable slightly, as your helper keeps up the forward pull on the brake-arm cradle.

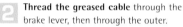 **Thread the greased cable** through the brake lever, then through the outer.

● Dribble a little oil into the outer.

● Make sure that the outer is firmly located in the lever, then thread the cable through the barrel adjuster and seat the outer firmly into it.

● Thread the cable through the cable-clamp bolt.

3 **Pull the cable backwards** with the long-nosed pliers while you push the brake-arm cradle forwards and hook the clamp bolt into it.

● Bend the cable slightly behind the clamp bolt and ask someone to push the brake-arm cradle forwards. Use your free hand to tighten up the bolt so the cable is nipped in place.

5 **Pull the brake lever hard** repeatedly (ten times) to bed in the brakes. The brakes may be a little tight as if they are being applied gently, even when there is no pressure on the lever.

● Keep about 15mm (²⁄₅in) of play in the brake lever before the brakes begin to bite.

6 **Screw in the barrel adjuster** a few turns until you achieve the 15mm (²⁄₅in) of play in the brake lever.

● Pull in the lever after each turn in the adjuster to check when the brakes begin to bite.

TUNING YOUR SUSPENSION

Suspension technology has revolutionized off-road riding. Accurate adjustment of the front fork and the rear shock allows uneven terrain to be tackled safely and confidently.

6

SUSPENSION FORKS

A suspension fork softens the blow of a bump on the road or trail. The fork must be checked for wear and lubricated regularly. The oil and springs should be changed either when they wear or to alter the characteristics of the fork.

How they work

The suspension fork on the front wheel absorbs the energy of a bump and prevents the force from reaching the rider. The fork's main spring, which can be trapped air or a metal coil, is compressed as the sliders move up the stanchions. Compression ends when the spring has absorbed the shock of the bump. At this point, the spring pushes the sliders back and the fork rebounds. Damping controls the speed of compression and rebound, usually by absorbing some of the energy of the bump with an air or oil damping mechanism. This creates friction, which slows down the fork's movements.

Reacting to bumps
Damping should prevent the fork from reaching the limits of its travel, but the fork should still be reactive enough to cope with every bump.

FRONT FORK COMPRESSION

Bunnyhopping gives a graphic demonstration of compression and rebound. As the rider picks up the front of the bike to clear the log, the fork rebounds because the rider's weight has been taken off the spring. On landing, the fork compresses as the spring absorbs the shock of the bike and rider landing.

Rebound

Pulling the handlebar upwards *and moving the body backwards lifts the front wheel so the front fork rebounds.*

Compression

Landing on the ground *returns the rider's weight to the bike's frame and compresses the front fork.*

AIR/OIL FORK

When a bump pushes up the sliders on this fork, a piston moves up the left stanchion, compressing the air. Once the bump has been absorbed, the air pushes the piston back and the fork rebounds. The damping mechanism in the right stanchion, which is full of oil, also moves up and down with the bump, controlling the speed of compression and rebound.

Fork crown
Turns the fork

Brake arch
Connects the two sliders

Seal
Keeps dirt out of fork's interior

Left stanchion
Contains the spring mechanism and piston

Right stanchion
Contains the damping mechanism

Air chamber
Contains air

Oil chamber
Contains oil

Damping mechanism
Moves up and down with slider

Piston
Moves up and down in response to bumps

Slider
Moves up and down on the stanchion

Shaft bolt
Fastens shaft to slider

Front suspension

A suspension fork works best if it has been set up to accommodate the rider's weight. When you sit on your bike, the amount the fork depresses, as the slider moves down the stanchion, is called the sag. As you ride, sag allows the fork to extend into the hollows in the ground, giving a smooth ride. To set the amount of sag, you can increase or decrease the amount of pre-load in the fork.

Damping controls the speed at which a fork works. To find out if a fork is working too fast, lean on the handlebar, then quickly lift up the front of the bike. If the suspension fork bangs back to its limit, its action is too quick and its rebound damping needs to be increased. Adjust the damping still further after a few rides. The best set-up will see the fork absorb a hit and rebound quickly enough to be ready for the next.

STEP LOCATOR

Parts of a suspension fork

Steerer
Air valve
Crown
Stanchion
Fork brace
Brake boss
Slider
Drop-out

Toolbox

- Shock pump ● Tie-wrap
- Tape measure

Setting sag

1 **Put a tie-wrap** around the stanchion of the unloaded fork and next to the top of the slider. Ideally, the sag should be about 25 per cent of its available travel, though cross-country riders often prefer less and downhillers more.

3 **Get off the bike** and carefully measure the distance between the tie-wrap and the top of the slider.

- Express this measurement as a proportion of the fork's available travel. If the distance is 25mm (1in) on an 80mm (3¹/₅in) fork, the proportion is 32 per cent. Check the owner's manual to find out the available travel of your bike.

Fine-tuning the fork

Sit on the bike, wearing your normal cycling clothes.

● Place both feet on the pedals. Either ask someone to hold you upright on the bike or lean your elbow against a wall. The slider will travel up the stanchion, pushing the tie-wrap with it.

Fine-tune the damping on some forks with an adjuster at the bottom of one of the fork legs. The two air chambers in this fork enable further refinements to damping to be made.

● Pump air into the bottom chamber with a shock pump to change the spring characteristics.

● Change the size of a valve on the air piston to control air flow between chambers. This flow is called air-damping.

Increase the air in the chamber with a shock pump if the proportion of available travel is greater than 25 per cent.

● Increase the spring pre-load with a coil/oil system (there is usually a dial at the top of the fork leg) or fit stronger springs.

● Release air, reduce the pre-load or fit lighter springs if the proportion is less than 25 per cent.

Make damping adjustments on some types of fork while riding the bike. The controls for these on-the-fly adjusters are usually marked "faster" and "slower" to indicate which direction to turn them in. It is also possible to lockout some forks. This means that you can stop their action if you are riding over a very smooth surface and do not need suspension.

Coil/oil fork

If the sag has been set up correctly (see pp.152–3) but the coil/oil fork keeps bottoming out – the fork reaches the full extent of its travel but the spring cannot compress any more – it will be necessary to fit heavier-duty springs. Conversely, if the fork only reacts to the bigger lumps and bumps, lighter springs should be fitted.

The method of changing springs is similar in most coil/oil forks, but check the manufacturer's manual to find the features of the fork on the bike in question. It may not be necessary to remove the fork leg from the fork crown; or a spring in both legs of the fork may need replacing; or one leg may incorporate the spring, while the other has the damping mechanism.

STEP LOCATOR

Parts of a coil/oil fork

- Steerer
- Fork crown
- Top cap
- Fork crown bolts
- Stanchion
- Fork brace
- Brake boss
- Slider
- Drop-out

Toolbox

- Spanner ● Allen key multi-tool
- Flat screwdriver

Setting up a coil/oil fork

1 **Remove the circlip** from around the rebound adjuster of the fork by prising it off with a flat screwdriver. Be very careful. Do not dig your screwdriver too far under the circlip, but put it far enough under so that it does not slip. Keep your fingers away from the screwdriver to avoid injuring yourself if it slips.

4 **Drop the** new spring into the fork leg. Make sure that it sits properly in the fork leg, then replace the top cap.

● Screw the top cap in with your fingers, then tighten it with a spanner.

2 **Undo the** retaining bolts in the fork crown so that you can drop the legs out. There are usually four retaining bolts. Some fork crowns do not have them, in which case undo a cap bolt at the top of the fork leg to remove the springs.

3 **Start to remove the top** cap of the fork leg with a spanner on the spanner flats, then unscrew the cap the rest of the way out with your fingers.

- Note how the spring is sitting in the fork leg, then lift the spring out.

5 **Put the** fork legs back in the fork crown and secure the retaining bolts.

- Follow the manufacturer's torque settings when replacing the retaining bolts.

- Reset the sag of your forks (see pp.152–3).

Air/oil fork

Air/oil suspension forks usually have short travel and are popular with cross-country riders. Their spring medium is air, which makes them very light, and their mechanism is damped by oil.

Sometimes, they have a negative spring working in the opposite direction to the main air spring. This helps to overcome the stiction (the sticky friction between two adjacent but motionless objects) which is inherent in air/oil suspension forks and is caused by their very tight seals.

Changing oil is necessary from time to time, as dirt in the system starts to cause excessive wear. If you have increased the damping on your fork and its action is still too fast, replacing the oil with a heavier one will slow them down. In the same way, lighter oil can help to speed them up.

STEP LOCATOR

Parts of an air/oil suspension fork

Steerer
Air valve
Fork crown
Fork brace
Stanchion
Brake boss
Slider
Drop-out

Toolbox

- Spanner
- Shock pump

Replacing oil

1 **Remove the cap** from the top of the stanchion without the Shrader air valve. This is the same sort of valve that is used on car tyres. You can carry out this following sequence of steps with the fork still in the bike, although it is easier if someone helps you.

3 **Make sure that you hold** the fork legs absolutely vertical.

- Place a bowl under the fork to catch any spillage. Carefully pour new oil into the stanchion until it is full and then replace the cap.

- Use a calibrated chemist's pouring vessel to ensure that you accurately measure the amount of oil, if the fork manufacturer specifies.

2 **Pour out the old oil** from the stanchion and collect it in a plastic cup. This air/oil fork has an open-bath damping system, where the damping rod moves up and down an open oil bath. The oil also lubricates the rest of the suspension system.

4 **Put the cap back** on the top of the oil stanchion and tighten it.

● Set the sag again (*see pp.152–3*), pumping air in or letting it out to obtain the ideal sag.

● Tighten the Schrader valve if, after setting up the sag correctly, your fork works well at first, then starts to bottom out (the valve may be leaking). Use a valve key from a car maintenance shop.

5 **Pump air in** or let air out of a fork with negative air springs after you have replaced the oil for one of a different viscosity.

● Adjust the damping of the fork so that it works at the speed you require, then fine-tune its action with the negative spring.

● Pump air in to make the fork more active over small bumps. Let air out to make it less responsive.

Lefty suspension

A Lefty houses its suspension and damping systems in a single leg, removing the need for the two legs of a traditional suspension fork. This prevents mud from clogging the front wheel – a useful thing to have on an off-road bike – and is lighter.

Removing and refitting the front wheel of a Lefty, cleaning the air filters, and cleaning and lubricating the telescopic leg are essential maintenance tasks. Further maintenance is best left to qualified technicians. The protective rubber boot should be checked for splits, and the system assessed to ensure it is functioning smoothly. Consult a technician if it is not.

STEP LOCATOR

Parts of a Lefty suspension unit

Rubber boot

Filter cover

Upper ring-clamps

Lower ring-clamp

Front brake-calliper

Wheel mounting bolt

Schrader valve

Toolbox

● Allen key multi-tool ● Insulator tape ● Rag and sponge for cleaning ● Grease ● Shock pump

Cleaning and greasing a Lefty

1 **Undo the two Allen bolts** that hold the front disc-brake calliper onto its mount.

● Carefully lift the calliper over the disc rotor and wrap its hose around the handlebar to keep it safely out of the way.

4 **Wash the filter** with soapy water on a sponge or cloth. Rinse it gently and pat it dry, then spray it with a little oil.

● Remove the tape covering the air holes, then carefully place the foam filter back under its rubber cover. Undo the bottom ring-clamp and slide the boot back up to the filter cover, then lap its top lip over the bottom edge of the cover. Secure both in place with the two ring-clamps.

2 **Undo the Allen bolt** in the centre of the hub while supporting the wheel in your other hand.

● Once the bolt is undone, carefully lift the wheel off the axle.

● To replace the wheel, carefully lift it onto the axle until you feel the bolt engage. Then tighten it with the Allen key and reverse Step 1 to re-fit the front calliper.

3 **Detach the two ring-clamps** at the top of the rubber boot by loosening the Allen bolts.

● Disengage the lower, longer section of the boot from the smaller top section, then slide the lower section down and secure it with the lower clamp.

● The top section of the boot is the filter cover. Slide it up and prise out the foam filter. This reveals two air holes, one on the front (*inset*) and one on the back of the leg – cover them with tape.

5 **Release the air** from the Lefty by depressing the Schrader valve located at the bottom of the leg (*inset*).

● Undo the ring-clamp at the bottom of the boot, then lift the boot. Wipe all the old grease from the leg with a dry cloth.

6 **Apply new grease**, either with a grease gun or brush. Spread it out as evenly as possible.

● Slide the boot back down the fork leg and re-attach it with the ring-clamp.

● Screw your shock pump on to the Schrader valve and re-inflate the fork to the personal settings as directed in the Lefty manual (*inset*).

Looking after suspension forks

Suspension forks soak up a lot of abuse because that is what they are designed to do. Although manufacturers do whatever they can to protect the inner workings, there are still some things you need to do to look after your forks.

Chief among them is cleaning. If you do not clean your forks regularly, dirt will wear down the seals at the top of the sliders and allow water to get into the inner workings and damage them. Worn seals will also allow oil to leak out, which affects the fork's performance.

Cleaning also gives you the opportunity to examine the forks for cracks and defects. You can also look for tell-tale signs of seal wear, such as the absence of a dirt ring on the stanchions after a ride – you should see this ring after every ride.

Another one of your regular jobs is to check the fork's settings. You can set the speed at which some forks work, along with other features. You need to check these settings have not been reset after a tough ride or after cleaning.

Do not use pressure hoses to clean suspension forks, as they can force water into the inner workings. You need to use a much gentler method of cleaning this part of your bike.

STEP LOCATOR

1 2 3 4 5 6

Toolbox
- Stiff-bristled brushes ● Sponge ● Oil
- Degreaser

Cleaning suspension forks

1 **Remove mud and dirt** with a dry, stiff-bristled brush. Remove the front wheel if there is a lot of mud on the fork, as it will make the job easier.

- Start at the top of the fork and brush downwards. Take care not to scrub too hard around the fork seals.

- Use smaller brushes to get into hard-to-reach places on the fork.

4 **Apply light, Teflon-based lubricant** to the seals at the top of the sliders to keep them supple and help maintain their integrity.

- Apply the oil sparingly but make sure you spread it all around the circumference of both seals.

- Avoid spilling oil on the tyres of your bike. If you do spill any, wash it off immediately with hot, soapy water.

2 **Spray degreaser** all over the fork, especially on the stanchions, to remove the old oil and dirt – a mix that could corrode the seals on your fork.

● Again, start spraying degreaser from the top of the fork and work downwards.

3 **Wipe the fork clean** with a clean sponge soaked in warm water. Wrap the sponge around the fork to ensure it gets completely rinsed. Start from the top and work down.

● Remove the wheel so you can give the lower part of the fork a thorough clean.

● Examine the fork for cracks and defects while you carry out this step.

5 **Pump the fork** up and down by pushing on the handlebars so that the seals become well coated.

● This is a good time to check for cracks on your handlebars and stem.

● Do not be tempted to alter the settings of the fork if it is hard to push. What matters is the way the fork feels when you ride.

6 **Check the settings dials** on your fork. Cleaning, especially when you use the stiff-bristled brush, can move the dials. Check they are set where you want them for riding.

● Check the cable outers or hoses for wear over the crown of the fork.

● As a final step, turn your bike upside down for five minutes to help redistribute the oil inside the fork.

REAR SUSPENSION

The rear suspension absorbs the shock caused by a bump in the ground or rough terrain. A shock absorber must be kept clean and lubricated, and the bushings and frame mounts checked regularly for damage and wear.

How it works

The shock absorber of the rear suspension mirrors the specifications of the front fork in order to increase the rider's control of the bike. The rear triangle of the frame, which connects the rear wheel to the shock absorber, can move independently of the rest of the frame on bikes that are fitted with rear suspension.

Shock absorbers, or shocks as they are also known, consist of a spring medium, either a coil or trapped air, and a shaft. The shaft is usually connected to a damping mechanism, which contains oil and controls the speed of the shock absorber's action.

COMPRESSION OF THE SHOCK ABSORBER

When the back wheel hits a bump on the road or trail, the rear triangle moves up on its pivots, compressing the spring, which absorbs the shock.

As the spring pushes back on the rear triangle of the frame, the shock rebounds, pushing the rear wheel back ready for the next bump.

When riding over smooth ground *the rear shock absorber is in a neutral position.*

When riding over rough ground *the rear shock is in a compressed position to absorb bumps.*

AIR/OIL SHOCK ABSORBER ANATOMY

In an air/oil shock absorber, the spring mechanism is compressed air that is sealed inside an air sleeve. The damping mechanism in the shock body contains oil. When the bike hits a bump, the shock body travels up inside the air sleeve and compresses the trapped air. Once this air spring has absorbed the energy of the bump, the shock absorber begins to rebound and return to its original position. The shaft, which runs from the top of the air sleeve into the shock body, is connected to the damping device. Oil flowing through holes in the device slows the action of the shock absorber in compression and rebound as the shock body travels up and down.

Bushing
Attaches shock to frame

Air valve
Controls air pressure in the sleeve

Rebound adjuster
Changes speed of rebound

Shaft
Runs into shock body

Air sleeve
Contains compressed air

Shock body
Contains the damping device

Rear shock
Absorbs the force of a bump

Rear triangle
Transmits the force of a bump to the rear shock

Rear wheel
Moves up and down in response to bumps

Rear suspension

A good-quality, full-suspension bike should be designed with a rear shock absorber that complements and works with the suspension fork in the front. Air/oil forks are normally accompanied by an air/oil shock and coil/oil systems are usually married together.

The first step in setting up a rear shock is to adjust its sag. Take into account the rider's weight, as with suspension forks (see pp.152–3), and then fine-tune its action by using damping and the shock's other functions after several rides on the bike.

One simple test to see if a rear shock is working in tune with the front fork is to press down on the middle of the bike, while looking at how the fork and shock react. For general riding, each should depress about the same amount.

Add the frame mounts, to which a shock is attached, to the routine safety checks (see pp.32–3). Check the bushings that allow the shock to pivot – consult the manufacturer's guide for instructions.

STEP LOCATOR

Parts of a rear suspension unit

Shock body

Pro-pedal adjuster

Air sleeve Air valve Rebound adjuster

Toolbox

• Tape measure • Shock pump

Adjusting the sag

1 **Measure the centre-to-centre** distance between the shock-mounting bolts, with the bike unloaded.

• Familiarize yourself with the valves and various controls of your shock before going further.

3 **To achieve the proportion of sag** that your riding style requires, let air out or pump it in as needed, then take the second measurement again.

• If your bike has a coil/oil shock, increase or decrease the pre-load to achieve the measurement you want. The recommended range is only a guide.

2 **Sit on the bike**
and ask someone to measure this distance again.

● Take both measurements and calculate the second as a percentage of the first. This will reveal the proportion of the shock's overall travel that is used as "sag". For general riding the figure should be between a quarter and a third.

● Cross-country racers tend to want stiffer shocks, so they sometimes go for a quarter or less.

● Downhill racers like their shocks to move a lot more. Their bikes often feel spongy to ride on the flat, but are really active when descending.

4 **Fine-tune the damping speed** of your shock with the rebound adjuster – if your bike has one.

● Turn the adjuster on an air/oil shock absorber but follow instructions on the shock to find out which way to turn.

● Do not set it too fast because this can upset the handling of the bike.

5 **Some shocks have additional** features. The pro-pedal system on this one allows you to control pedal-induced movement of the shock.

● Familiarize yourself with your shock's features by reading the instruction manual.

● Ride your bike across different terrains and see what happens when you vary the settings. Knowing all about your bike and the way you ride will help you get the best out of any trail situation.

Looking after rear suspension

Rear suspension comes in many forms, but most designs have a rear triangle that pivots on the main frame of the bike, its movement controlled by a shock absorber situated between the rear triangle and the main frame. This allows the rear wheel to move up and down, absorbing shocks while remaining in contact with the ground.

The pivots are mounted on bearings or bushings for smooth movement. Occasionally these components require lubrication, and will eventually wear out. Check the Servicing timetable (*see pp.42–3*) for when to lubricate. To test for wear you will need to inspect the bearings and check for play at the pivots from time to time.

STEP LOCATOR

Parts of bushings and bearings

Bearing cover

| Small bushing | Large bushing | Small bearing | Large bearing |

Toolbox

● Allen key multi-tool ● Flat-head screwdriver
● Spray degreaser, grease ● Rubber mallet or metal-headed hammer ● Drift to fit bearings

Servicing bearings and bushings

1 **To expose the pivot bearing,** you may need to remove any linkage arms.

● In this case, the linkage arm is attached to the bearing on which it pivots by an Allen bolt. Remove the pivot-bolt with an Allen key, then unhook the linkage.

● Linkages are often bolted together while under load, so you may need someone to help you loosen it by applying counter pressure.

4 **Thoroughly clean** the inside of the bearing seat – the hole where the bearing sits.

● Offer up the new bearing and place the drift squarely on top of it.

Use a flat–head screwdriver to carefully lift the cover from the bearing (*inset*). This reveals the ball bearings inside.

● Flush out any old dirt and lube with a spray degreaser, then apply new grease to the ball bearings with a grease gun or brush. Apply the grease sparingly but evenly.

● Replace the bearing cover, ensuring it is seated firmly in place, then reverse Step 1 to replace any linkage arms.

To replace a worn bearing, first detach any linkage arms by undoing the Allen pivot-bolt.

● With the arm and bolt removed, place a drift firmly and flush on to the bearing (*inset*).

● Sharply but carefully tap the drift with a rubber mallet – the bearing should emerge from the other side of the linkage. If the bearing doesn't move, you may need to use a metal-headed hammer to better concentrate the force.

Use your mallet to administer sharp but carefully aimed blows, square-on to the head of the drift.

● As with removing the old bearing, be patient – bearings must be a tight fit. Once the bearing is home, replace the pivot bolt and linkage. Again, you may require help to apply counter pressure.

Lubricate any pivot bushings, which are sometimes used on full–suspension bikes.

● These are maintained by occasionally applying thin oil where the two faces contact.

● Like bearings, bushings can also be replaced when worn out. Remove any linkage arms to expose the old bushing, then prise it out with a flat–head screwdriver. Clean the bushing seat and press in the new one.

Glossary

Terms in *italic* within an entry are defined under their own headings within the glossary.

ALLEN BOLT A threaded bolt with a hexagonal depression in the centre of its head.

ALLEN KEY Hexagonal-shaped tool that fits *Allen bolts*.

BEARING A mechanism that usually consists of a number of ball-bearings and circular channels, or races. It allows two metal surfaces to move freely while in contact.

BLOCK Sprockets fitted to a *freewheel*.

BOSS Threaded metal fixture on a bicycle frame to which an item such as a bottle cage or a pannier rack is attached.

BOTTOM BRACKET Rotating unit that connects the *cranks* on either side of the bottom bracket shell to each other.

BOTTOM OUT A term that describes the point when a *suspension* fork or shock absorber reaches the limit of its *travel*.

BRAKE-LEVER HOOD The body in which the brake lever sits, connecting it to the handlebar.

BRAKE TRAVEL The distance a brake lever moves before the brake pads engage the braking surface on the rim or hub of a wheel.

CABLE TIDY A small, soft-metal cylinder that is closed at one end and fits over the cut ends of a cable to prevent fraying.

CASSETTE *Sprockets* that fit on the *freehub*.

CHAINRING A toothed ring

attached to the *cranks*, which drives the chain and, in turn, the *sprockets* and the rear wheel of a bicycle.

CHAINSET The assembly of *chainrings* and *cranks*.

CHAINSTAY The frame tube joining the *bottom bracket* shell and rear *drop-out*.

CLEAT A plastic or metal plate that fits to the sole of a cycling shoe and engages into a *clipless pedal* to hold the foot on the pedal.

CLIPLESS PEDAL A pedal with a mechanism to engage the *cleat* on the sole of a cycling shoe and hold it securely in place. Called clipless because they replaced pedals that had toe clips and straps.

COG A circular metal object with teeth, sometimes used as an alternative term for *sprocket*. It usually describes the parts within a hub gear that can be combined to give different gear ratios.

COMPRESSION The action of a *suspension* system when it absorbs an impact from the terrain. The term refers to the compression of the spring.

CRANK The lever that joins the pedals to the *chainrings* and transfers energy from the rider's legs into the *drivetrain* of the bike.

DAMPING The process that absorbs the energy of an impact transmitted through a *suspension* system. It controls the speed at which any form of suspension responds to uneven terrain.

DERAILLEUR GEARS A system that shifts the chain between

sprockets on the rear wheel (rear derailleur) and between *chainrings* attached to *cranks* (front derailleur); it allows multiple gearing on bikes. See also *Mech*.

DOWN TUBE The frame tube that joins the *bottom-bracket* shell to the *head tube*.

DRIVETRAIN The assembly of pedals, *chainset*, chain, and *sprockets* that drives the bike forwards by transmitting leg power into wheel rotation. See also *Transmission*.

DROP-OUT A slotted plate at the end of the fork legs and stays, into which the axle of a wheel is attached.

EXPANDER BOLT A bolt that draws up a truncated cone or triangle of metal inside a metal tube in order to wedge the tube in place. Commonly found inside the stem of a threaded *headset*.

FREEHUB A mechanism, part of the hub, that allows the rear wheel to rotate while the pedals remain stationary.

FREEWHEEL A mechanism that does the same job as a *freehub* but can be screwed on or off the hub.

GEAR An expression of the *chainring* and *sprocket* combination, linked by the chain, that propels the bike.

GEAR SATELLITE A disc on a hub gear that rotates when the gear cable is shifted, moving the cogs within the hub to change gear.

GEAR-SHIFTER The control mechanism, usually on the handlebar, used to initiate gear-shifts.

GPS Global Positioning System, a satellite-based navigational network used in cycling for navigation and to record speed and other ride data, via a handlebar-mounted device.

GRUB SCREW A headless, threaded bolt with a single diameter throughout its length.

HEADSET The *bearing* unit that attaches the forks to a frame and allows them to turn. There are two varieties: threaded and threadless.

HEAD TUBE The frame tube through which the *steerer tube* runs.

HEXAGONAL BOLT OR NUT A threaded bolt with a hexagonal-shaped head, or a hexagonal-shaped nut that fits on to a threaded bolt.

HYDRAULIC A mechanical system that uses compressed fluid to move an object.

LOCKRING/LOCKNUT A ring or nut used to tighten on to a threaded object and lock it in place.

MECH Short for mechanism. Device that pushes the chain on to a larger or smaller *chainring* or *sprocket*. See also *Derailleur gears*.

NEGATIVE SPRING A device that works against the main spring in a *suspension* system. In compression, for example, a negative spring works to extend the fork, helping to overcome the effects of *stiction*.

NIPPLE The piece of metal attached to the end of a cable that secures the cable in the control lever.

PLAY A term to describe any looseness in mechanical parts.

QUICK-RELEASE MECHANISM A lever connected to a skewer that locks or releases a component from the frame.

REBOUND A term to describe the action of a *suspension* system after it absorbs an impact from the terrain. It refers to the extension of the system's spring.

SEAT POST A hollow tube that holds the saddle and is inserted into the *seat tube*.

SEAT STAY The frame tube joining the *bottom bracket* shell and rear *drop-out*.

SEAT TUBE The frame tube that holds the *seat post*.

SIDEWALL Part of the tyre between the *tread* and rim.

SPROCKET A *cog* turned by the chain. Combined with other sprockets, it forms a *cassette* or *block*.

STEERER TUBE The tube that connects the fork to the *stem* and handlebar.

STEM The component that connects the handlebar to the *steerer tube*.

STICTION A term that combines the words static and friction. It describes the tension between moving and static parts at rest, such as the seals and stanchions in a *suspension* fork.

STOPPER PIN The end of a cantilever or V-brake return spring that fits into a locating hole on the bike's brake mounting *bosses*.

SUSPENSION An air/oil or a coil/oil system that absorbs the bumps from a trail or road. The system is either integrated into the fork or connected to the rear wheel via a linkage.

THREADS The spiral grooves cut into metal that allow separate parts to be screwed or bolted together.

TOP TUBE The frame tube that joins the *seat tube* to the *head tube*.

TRANSMISSION A bike's transmission is made up of those parts that transfer the rider's energy into forward motion – the pedals, chain, *chainset* and *sprockets*. See also *Drivetrain*.

TRAVEL A term that refers to the total distance a component moves in carrying out its purpose. For example, travel in a *suspension* fork is the total distance the fork has available to move in order to absorb a shock.

TREAD The central part of a tyre that makes contact with the ground.

VISCOSITY A rating system for oils, which also refers to the weight. A light oil has low viscosity and moves quicker than a heavy oil through a given *damping* mechanism. This results in a faster-acting *suspension* system or reduced damping.

WHEEL JIG A stand that holds a wheel so that its rim runs between two jaws. Used in truing a wheel after replacing a broken spoke.

Index

A

accessories 26–27
air/oil forks 151–53
    bottoms out 44–45
    damping 156, 157
    oil replacement 156–57
    parts 156
    Schrader valve 157
    shock absorber, anatomy
      163
    see also suspension forks
Allen keys 33, 34, 168
    aluminium frame, rivets,
      protection from 41
    anatomy of bike 12–13
    anti-seize compound, seat
      pin and stem 39

B

bag, under-saddle 27
band-on, front mech 62
bar-end gear cable
    parts 56
    replacing 56–57
barrel adjuster
    brake 123, 133, 141, 146
    gear cable 58, 59
    mech, rear 64
    bearing-puller tools, bottom
      bracket 86–87
bearings 38, 168
bench vice 33
BMX bike 18, 19
    U-brakes, maintenance and
      adjustment 134–35
bolts, servicing 42
bottle cage 26
bottom bracket 168
    bearing-puller tools 86–87
    cartridge 82–83
    cartridge-bearing anatomy
      80
    crank removal 83, 86
    hollow-axle anatomy 81

    hollow-axle replacement
      84–85
    Italian-threaded 83
    lubrication 38
    maintenance 82–83, 86–87
    press-fit 86–87
    press-fit, anatomy of 86
    servicing 43
    Shimano Octalink 82
    square-tapered 82–83
    tools 33
    types 82
    workings of 80
    see also chainset
brake
    barrel adjuster 123, 133,
      141, 146
    bike front diving under
      braking 44–45
    calliper see calliper brake
    Campagnolo brake/shift,
      securing 106
    cantilever see cantilever
      brake
    disc see disc brake
    fluid, draining and replacing,
      hydraulic disc brake
      144–45
    hose, split or leaking 46
    hub-mounted see
      hub-mounted brake
    hydraulic disc see hydraulic
      disc brake
    pre-ride checks 40
    problems 44–45
    reach 21
    rim, and wheel removal
      114–15
    roller brake see roller brake
    and safety 122
    servicing 42, 43
    straddle wire 132
    U-brake, maintenance and
      adjustment 134–35
    V-brake see V-brake
    see also wheels
brake cable 122

    adjustment, brake reach 21
    cutting outers 34
    disc 142
    replacement, drop handlebar
      124–25
    replacement, straight
      handlebar 126–27
    split or frayed 47
    travel adjustment,
      hub-mounted brake
      140–41
brake lever 105, 106–07,
    126
    anatomy 123
    gear shifter combination 53
    hub-mounted brake 137
    play in 44–45
    road bike, optimum position
      23
brake pads
    adjustment, calliper brake
      128, 129
    adjustment cantilever brake
      132–33
    adjustment, side-pull
      calliper brake 135
    adjustment, U-brake 135
    adjustment, V-brake 130,
      131
    ineffective 44–45
    servicing 42, 43
    uneven contact 44–45
    wear, checking for uneven
      46
    wheel removal 114–15
    wheel rim contact 122–23
bumps, reacting to 150–51
bunnyhopping 150

C

cable
    brake see brake cable
    cutters 33
    cutting outers 34
    gear see gear cable
    lubrication 38–39, 45, 63
    mech see mech cable

Acknowledgments

Author's acknowledgments

Pip Morgan and Richard Gilbert for their patient and diplomatic editorial work.

Ted Kinsey for designing everything so that the writing makes sense.

Dave Marsh of the Universal Cycle Centre for technical advice regarding road bikes.

Wayne Bennett of Don't Push It Mountain Bikes for advice regarding mountain bikes.

Tim Flooks of TF Tuned Shox for advice regarding suspension.

Gerard Brown for his excellent pictures and Guy Andrews for getting together the equipment we needed to show all the aspects of bike maintenance.

Jo Jackson and Keith and Barbara Oldfield for help when the author's computer broke down, twice.

Finally, all the bike companies who lent their equipment for our photoshoots.

Publisher's acknowledgments

Original edition produced by:
Senior Art Editor Kevin Ryan,
Art Editor Michael Duffy,
Managing Editor Adèle Hayward,
Managing Art Editor Karen Self,
Category Publisher Stephanie Jackson, Art Director Peter Luff,
DTP Designers Rajen Shah, Adam Shepherd, Production Controller Kevin Ward

Design: Janice English, Simon Murrell, Dawn Young

DTP Design: Gemma Casajuana

Photoshoot Art Director: Jo Grey

Picture Research: Carolyn Clerkin

Proofreading: Lynn Bresler

Illustrations: Kevin Jones and Matthew White at Kevin Jones Associates, Tim Loughead at Precision Illustration Ltd.

Additional photography: Jill and Steve Behr at Stockfile

Models: Jay Black, Chris Hopkins, James Millard, Simon Oon, Helen Rosser, Rochele Whyte

Cycling models: Hsu Minh Chung, Jamie Newell, Claire Paginton, Hannah Reynolds, Simon Richardson, Kelli Salone, Ross Tricker, Russell Williams

Accessory, component, and bicycle suppliers:
Ian Young at Moore Large for Schwinn BMX; Caroline Griffiths at Madison for Profile, Shimano, Finish Line, Park, Ridgeback, Cervelo, and Commencal; Ross Patterson and Jon Holdcroft at ATB sales for Electra and Marin bikes; Collette Clensy at Giant Bikes; Adrian at Pashley bicycles; Evans Cycles in Wandsworth and Milton Keynes; Cedric at Luciano Cycles, Clapham; Sam at Bikepark, Covent Garden; Richard at Apex Cycles, Clapham; Graham at SRAM; Shelley at Continental; Trek UK; Mike Cotty at Cannondale; Richard Pascoe of Ricci—Bike Chain; Fisher Outdoor Leisure; Mark Haylett at Specialized; and Gary Anderson at Chicken Cycle-Kit.

Picture credits

The publisher would like to thank the following for their kind permission to reproduce their photographs:

56—7: Stockfile/Steve Behr;
150: Fox Racing Shox.

All other images © DK Images.

For further information see www.dkimages.com

PLEASE NOTE

Bicycle maintenance is potentially hazardous. Whilst the information in this book has been prepared with the reader's personal safety in mind, the reader may help to reduce the inherent risks involved by following these instructions precisely. The scope of this book allows for some, but not all, the potential hazards and risks to be explained to the reader. Therefore, the reader is advised to adopt a careful and cautious approach when following the instructions, and if in any doubt, to refer to a good bike shop or specialist.